SRA
Reading
Success
Effective Comprehension Strategies

Student Workbook
Foundations

McGraw Hill **SRA**

Columbus, OH

SRAonline.com

 SRA

Send all inquiries to this address:
SRA/McGraw-Hill
4400 Easton Commons
Columbus, OH 43219

ISBN: 978-0-07-618480-4
MHID: 0-07-618480-3

    5 6 7 8 9 10 MAL 13 12 11

The **McGraw·Hill** *Companies*

Lesson 1

Part A - Asking Questions: Introduction

If you ask yourself questions *while* you are reading, it helps you remember what you have read. You can ask yourself many questions about even a short passage.

> Canada is a large country located north of the United States. Instead of states, Canada has provinces. There are ten provinces in Canada.

Here are some questions you can ask yourself about this short passage:

1. Where is Canada?

2. What size is Canada?

3. Canada is located in which direction from the United States?

4. What is Canada?

5. How many provinces are there in Canada?

6. What does Canada have instead of states?

7. What does the United States have instead of provinces?

Part B - Asking Questions

Directions: Read the short passage below. Write as many questions about the passage as you can think of. Your teacher will call on some students to read their questions and others to answer them.

> One of Canada's provinces is also an island. It is called Prince Edward Island and it is small. Prince Edward Island is about 2,185 square miles in size. That makes it the smallest province in Canada. Part of another province is also an island. The name of that province is Newfoundland and Labrador. The "Newfoundland" part of that province is an island. It is much larger than Prince Edward Island. Newfoundland is pronounced "NEW fund lund." Both provinces are in the far eastern part of Canada.

_____

_____

_____

_____

_____

Part C- Literal Questions: Introduction

The most basic type of question to ask yourself when you read is a **literal** question. The answer to a **literal** question is found in the passage you are reading. The questions listed in Part A are **literal** questions.

Example: Read the sentence below, paying special attention to the underlined part. Next, read the **literal** question below the sentence.

The soccer club is having a car wash at the school tomorrow, at <u>three in the afternoon</u>.

Here is a **literal** question about the underlined part:

At what time will the car wash be?

Sometimes there are different ways to write the answer found in the passage:

3:00 pm
three o'clock in the afternoon
3 in the afternoon

Part D- Literal Questions

Directions: Read the paragraph below. Next, answer the literal questions. NOTE: There are TWO correct answers to each question.

Canada is the second largest country in the world. Its population is about thirty-two million. That is not a very large number of people. It is about same as the state of California. California is only 1/25 the size of Canada. Most Canadians live within about 200 miles of the border with the United States.

Mark the TWO correct answers to each question.

1. Canada is the:
    a.   biggest country in the Southern Hemisphere
    b.   2nd largest country in the world
    c.   largest country in the world
    d.   one of the largest countries in the world

2. The population of Canada is about:
    a.   32,000,000
    b.   320,000,000
    c.   32 billion
    d.   the same as California

3. The majority of Canadians live:
    a.   in Newfoundland and Labrador
    b.   within about two hundred miles of the United States
    c.   near California
    d.   pretty close to the United States

Part E- Memory Techniques

It is easier to remember something if you relate that thing to other things. Based on what you have read, write "Newfoundland and Labrador" next to the correct arrow on the map below, and then write "Prince Edward Island" next to the correct arrow.

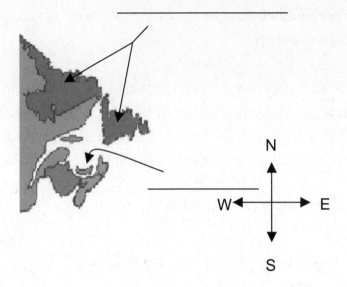

Part F- Bonus

One meaning of **detail** is "a small part of something." The "something" could be a building, for example. The details of a building could be parts like the doors and the windows, the design of the bricks on the outside, and other parts--all smaller than the building.

A **detail** in a reading passage is a small part of the passage. You have read short passages about Canada in this lesson. Canada is "the whole thing" talked about in the passage. In these passages, the **details** are the facts about Canada.

The word **detail** comes from a Latin word that means "cut." **Detail** is related to the word tailor "someone who cuts cloth" (and then sews it together).

Detail will be a bonus item on some quizzes or tests that you take.

Optional Prosody Exercise

Part G - Reading Aloud

Directions: Listen to your teacher read the sentences below. Your teacher will read them so that they sound like normal English when it is spoken. If your teacher calls on you to read one of the

sentences, try to read it so that it sounds like someone speaking. Take your time. You can read the sentence silently before reading it aloud.

1. There are ten provinces in Canada.

2. Canada is the second largest country in the world.

3. What is Prince Edward Island?

4. The word **detail** comes from a Latin word that means "cut."

Lesson 2

Part A - Reviewing Details

Directions: Follow your teacher's instructions.

1. Name the province of Canada that is also an island.

_____

2. Where is Canada located?

_____

3. Canada has about as many people as the US state of:

_____

4. Where do most Canadians live?

_____

5. The provinces in Canada are like _____ in the United States.

_____

Part B - Asking Questions

Directions: Read the short passage below. Write as many questions about the passage as you can think of. Your teacher will call on some students to read their questions and others to answer them.

As you have read, Canada has ten provinces. Each province is like one of the fifty states in the United States. The smallest province in Canada is Prince Edward Island. Because the name of that province is long, people in Canada usually refer to it by an abbreviation, P.E.I. Prince Edward Island is an island as well as a province. Another province in the eastern part of Canada is called Newfoundland and Labrador. Newfoundland is also an island. Labrador is part of the mainland.

_____

_____

_____

_____

_____

Part C- Literal Questions

Remember, the most basic type of question to ask yourself when you read is a **literal** question. The answer to a **literal** question is found in the passage you are reading.

Sometimes there are different ways to write the answer found in the passage.

Part D- Literal Questions

Directions: Read the paragraph below. Next, answer the literal questions. NOTE: There are TWO correct answers to each question.

Canada has ten provinces. The province furthest west is called British Columbia. The province furthest east is Newfoundland and Labrador.

Mark the TWO correct answers to each question.

1. Canada has _____ provinces:
   a. fifty
   b. ten
   c. 10
   d. 50

2. British Columbia is:
   a. furthest East
   b. in the West
   c. the smallest province
   d. furthest West

3. Newfoundland and Labrador is:
   a. furthest East
   b. in the East
   c. an island
   d. furthest West

Part E- Memory Techniques

It is easier to remember something if you relate that thing to other things. How can you remember that Canada has about 32,000,000 people, instead of, for example, 320,000,000 or 32,000? The population of the United States is about 250,000,000 and you know there are fewer people in Canada. Therefore, 320,000,000 is way too much. On the other hand, 32,000 is less than the number of people who attend many major league baseball games. It is way too small.

Part F- Bonus

One meaning of **detail** is "a small part of something." The passage below is mostly about the territories of Canada.

> In addition to provinces, Canada has three very large territories. The territories belong to Canada, but the government of a territory is different from that of a province. The three territories are: Yukon, Northwest Territories, and Nunavut. All three territories are north of the Canadian provinces.

The **details** are little facts about the territories of Canada, such as:

1. There are three territories.

2. The government of the territories is different from the government of the provinces.

3. The names of the territories are Yukon, Northwest Territories, and Nunavut.

4. All three territories are north of Canadian provinces.
Detail will be a bonus item on some quizzes or tests that you take.

Optional Prosody Exercise

Part G - Reading Aloud

Directions: Listen to your teacher read the sentences below. Your teacher will read them so that they sound like normal English when it is spoken. If your teacher calls on you to read one of the sentences, try to read it so that it sounds like someone speaking. Take your time. You can read the sentence silently before reading it aloud.

1. It is easier to remember something if you relate that thing to other things.

2. Where is Canada located?

3. Another province in the eastern part of Canada is called Newfoundland and Labrador.

4. Which province is also an island?

Lesson 3

Part A - Reviewing Details

Directions: Follow your teacher's instructions.

1. Is British Columbia the Canadian province that is furthest to the west or furthest to the east?

   _____

2. How many provinces does Canada have?

   _____

3. Canada has about as many people as the US state of:

   _____

4. Where do most Canadians live?

   _____

5. P.E.I. is an abbreviation for which Canadian province?

   _____

6. What is the second largest country in the world?

   _____

Part B - Asking Questions

Directions: Read the short passage below. Write as many questions about the passage as you can think of. Your teacher will call on some students to read their questions and others to answer them.

One of Canada's ten provinces is called British Columbia. You have read that British Columbia is the province that is furthest west in Canada. Just east of British Columbia there is another province called Alberta. British Columbia and Alberta are very large provinces. Prince Edward Island is very small. It is in the east.

_____

_____

_____

_____

_____

_____

Part C- Literal Questions

Directions: Read the paragraph below. Next, answer the literal questions. NOTE: There are TWO correct answers to each question.

Canada is the second largest country in the world. The largest country in the world is Russia. Even though it is big, the population of Canada is pretty small. There are 32,000,000 people in Canada. That is about the number of people in the U.S. state of California.

Mark the TWO correct answers to each question.

1. Canada is the _____ largest country in the world.

    a. third

    b. second

    c. 3rd

    d. 2nd

2. Russia is the _____ largest country in the world.

    a. 1st

    b. 2nd

    c. second

    d. first

3. There are about _____ people in Canada.

    a. thirty-two million

    b. 32,000,000

    c. three hundred twenty thousand

    d. 320,000

Part D- Memory Techniques

It is easier to remember something if you relate that thing to other things. Based on what you have read, write the names of provinces next to the correct arrows on the map below.

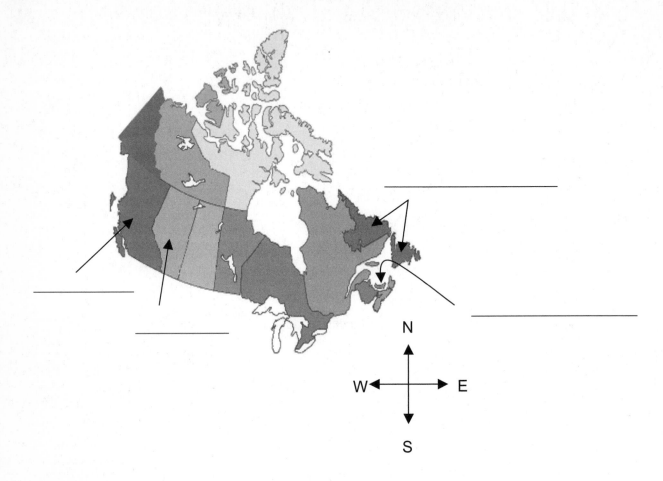

Part E- Bonus

One meaning of **detail** is "a small part of something." **Details** are little facts about something. **Detail** will be a bonus item on some quizzes or tests that you take.

Optional Prosody Exercise

Part F - Reading Aloud

Directions: Listen to your teacher read the sentences below. If your teacher calls on you to read one of the sentences, try to read it so that it sounds like someone speaking. Take your time. You can read the sentence silently before reading it aloud.

1. How may provinces does Canada have?

2. Next, answer the literal questions.

3. One meaning of **detail** is "a small part of something."

4. There are 32,000,000 people in Canada.

Lesson 4

Part A - Reviewing Details

Directions: Follow your teacher's instructions.

1. Which Canadian province is next to British Columbia?

_____

2. About how many people live in Canada?

_____

3. What is the largest country in the world?

_____

4. Which part of Newfoundland and Labrador is an island?

_____

5. What is the abbreviation for Prince Edward Island?

_____

6. Which Canadian province is furthest east?

_____

Part B - Asking Questions

Directions: Read the short passage below. Write as many questions about the passage as you can think of. Your teacher will call on some students to read their questions and others to answer them.

So far, you have read about four Canadian provinces. British Columbia and Alberta are in the western part of Canada. Prince Edward Island and Newfoundland and Labrador are in the eastern part. A fifth province is Nova Scotia. It is also in the east. The name "Nova Scotia" means "New Scotland" in Latin. The Scots were the first British people to settle there. Nova Scotia is a peninsula. ("Insula" is related to the word "island.") A peninsula is a body of land that is *almost* surrounded completely by water.

_____

_____

_____

_____

_____

Part C- Literal Questions

Directions: Read the paragraph below. Next, answer the literal questions. NOTE: There are TWO correct answers to each question.

Most of the people in Canada live close to the United States. Many live within two hundred miles of the border between the United States and Canada. That means that most people in Canada live in the southern part of the large provinces. The smallest province is Prince Edward Island. In Prince Edward Island most people live in Charlottetown. Charlottetown is the capital city of Prince Edward Island.

Mark the TWO correct answers to each question.

1. Which Canadian province is the smallest?
    a. Nova Scotia
    b. Prince Edward Island
    c. New Scotland
    d. P.E.I.

2. Most Canadians live within about _____ miles of the border between Canada and the United States.
    a. 200
    b. two hundred
    c. ten
    d. 10

3. In the large provinces of Canada, most people live in the
    a. north
    b. southern part
    c. south
    d. northern part

Part D- Memory Techniques

It is easier to remember something if you relate that thing to other things. Based on what you have read, write the names of provinces next to the correct arrows on the map below.

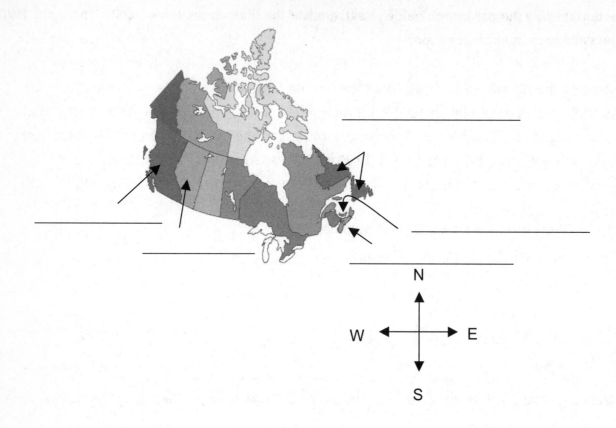

Part E- Bonus

One meaning of **detail** is "a small part of something." **Details** are little facts about something. **Detail** will be a bonus item on some quizzes or tests that you take.

Optional Prosody Exercise

Part F - Reading Aloud

Directions: Listen to your teacher read the sentences below. If your teacher calls on you to read one of the sentences, try to read it so that it sounds like someone speaking. Take your time. You can read the sentence silently before reading it aloud.

1. Many people live within two hundred miles of the border with the United States.

2. What is the abbreviation for Prince Edward Island?

3. "Insula" is related to the word "island."

4. What is the largest country in the world?

Lesson 5

Optional Prosody Exercise

Part C - Reading Aloud

Directions: Listen to your teacher read the sentences below. If your teacher calls on you to read one of the sentences, try to read it so that it sounds like someone speaking. Take your time. You can read the sentence silently before reading it aloud.

1. What Canadian province is the furthest *west?*

2. After you read the passage, you will stop and write questions about what you just read.

3. Humans belong to what class of vertebrates?

4. Mammals have hair or fur on their bodies to help keep them warm.

Lesson 6

Part A- Vocabulary: Words in Context

The following passage has a word missing. You can probably figure out what that word should be, however, because there are clues about the word in the sentences.

Our dog is harmless, but she _____ loudly at strangers. That makes her a pretty good watchdog.

You know what dogs might do that would scare strangers. The dog **barks** at strangers.

Part B- Vocabulary: Words in Context

Directions: Choose the word that would best fill in the blank for each sentence.

1. We heard a storm was coming. I was not happy because I don't like thunder, but I especially don't like _____.

    a. lightning

    b. news

    c. storms

2. Because of the drought, few people are watering their _____. That's okay with me because I don't like to mow and trim.

    a. flowers

    b. vegetables

    c. lawns

3. James doesn't have a single _____. He doesn't collect baseball cards, or listen to music, or build models, or anything like that.

    a. free minute

    b. hobby

    c. penny

Part C - Asking Questions

Directions: Read the short passage below. Write as many questions about the passage as you can think of. Your teacher will call on some students to read their questions and others to answer them.

You have read about five Canadian provinces: British Columbia, Alberta, Newfoundland and Labrador, Prince Edward Island, and Nova Scotia. Canada has ten provinces altogether. Another province is called New Brunswick. New Brunswick is near Nova Scotia. The provinces of Nova Scotia and New Brunswick are called *maritime* provinces. That means there is a lot of shipping and boating in the ports of those provinces. Prince Edward Island is also a *maritime* province. The French settled in the area where the *maritime* provinces are now and called that area

Acacia. The western border of New Brunswick is with the American state, Maine. All three *maritime* provinces have many hilly areas called *highlands.*

_____

_____

_____

_____

_____

Part D- Memory Techniques

Based on what you have read, write the names of the Canadian provinces next to the correct arrows on the map below.

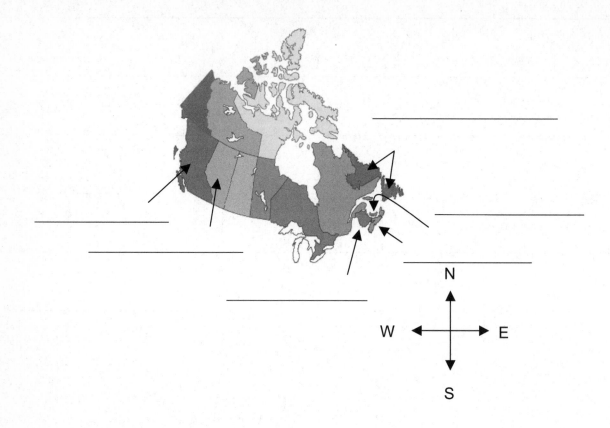

Part E- Remembering What You Read

Directions: Answer the questions about Canada below. Try to remember the answers without looking back on your worksheet.

1. How many provinces does Canada have?

2. How many *maritime provinces* does Canada have?

    a. ten

    b. three

    c. thirteen

3. What does Nova Scotia mean?

    a. Latin

    b. maritime provinces

    c. New Scotland

    d. Acacia

4. British Columbia and Alberta are _____ provinces.

    a. small

    b. large

    c. maritime

    d. Russian

5. Which Canadian province is also an island?

    a. Nova Scotia

    b. British Columbia

    c. Prince Edward Island

    d. Newfoundland and Labrador

6. *Part* of _____and Labrador is an island.

    a. British Columbia

    b. New Brunswick

    c. Prince Edward Island

    d. Newfoundland

7. Which province is NOT a maritime province?

    a. Alberta

    b. New Brunswick

    c. Nova Scotia

    d. Prince Edward Island

Part F- Bonus

The bonus word for this lesson is **inference**.

Inference is pronounced like this:

    IN•fur•unse

Inference means "guessing about something from another thing that you already know." When you read, you often have to **infer** something that isn't told to you directly in the passage.

Inference comes from Latin.

Inference will be a bonus item on some quizzes or tests that you take. To learn **inference,** you will have to know what it means, how to spell it, and where it comes from.

Bonus Review

Remember, a detail in a reading passage is a small part of the passage. The word detail comes from a Latin word that means "cut."

Optional Prosody Exercise

Part G - Reading Aloud

Directions: Listen to your teacher read the sentences below. If your teacher calls on you to read one of the sentences, try to read it so that it sounds like someone speaking. Take your time. You can read the sentence silently before reading it aloud.

1. How many *maritime* provinces does Canada have?

2. The French settled in the area where the *maritime* provinces are now and called that area *Acacia.*

3. You know what dogs might do that would scare strangers.

Lesson 7

Part A- Vocabulary: Words in Context

Directions: Choose the best word to fill in the blank for each sentence.

1. The _____ was running very high. We were afraid it might overflow its banks.

     a. cost

     b. river

     c. cloud

2. That fruit has been sitting in the sun so long that it is sure to _____, if it hasn't already. Then it's really going to stink.

    a. be stolen

    b. spoil

    c. ripen

3. Many people are complaining lately about the _____, even though the leaders were elected by a large majority.

    a. food

    b. weather

    c. government

Part B - Literal Questions

Directions: Read the paragraph below. Next, answer the literal questions. NOTE: There is only ONE correct answer to each question.

There are five lakes in North America called the **Great Lakes**. The names of the lakes from west to east are: Lake Superior, Lake Michigan, Lake Huron, Lake Erie, and Lake Ontario. All of Lake Michigan is in the United States. The other four lakes share borders with Canada and eight American states. The Canadian province of Ontario is the one that borders the Great Lakes. The lakes are all connected to one another.

1. How many Great Lakes are there?

_____

2. Which Great Lake is all inside the United States?

_____

3. Which Canadian province borders all the Great Lakes except for Lake Michigan?

_____

4. What do you call the five very large lakes in North America?

_____

5. Which lake is furthest to the west?

_____

6. Which lake is furthest to the east?

_____

Part C - Memory Techniques

Directions: Look at the list of Great Lakes below. Notice that when you list the Great Lakes in this order, the first letters spell "HOMES." If you can remember "HOMES," that will help you remember the names of the Great Lakes.

Huron
Ontario
Michigan
Erie
Superior

Part D- Remembering What You Read

Directions: Answer the questions about Canada below. Try to remember the answers without looking back on your worksheet.

1. The Maritime provinces of Canada are Nova Scotia, P.E.I., and:

_____

2. New Brunswick borders which American state?

    a. Michigan

    b. Maine

    c. Washington

3. Which province listed below is very large?

    a. Alberta

    b. P.E.I.

    c. Nova Scotia

Part E- Bonus

Remember, **inference** is pronounced like this:

    IN•fur•unse

Inference means "guessing about something from another thing that you already know."

Look at this question: "Which of the Great Lakes is the largest?"

The passage in Part B doesn't tell you the answer to that question. You might be able to **infer** the answer, though, by looking at the names of the lakes and then taking a guess.

Huron

Ontario

Michigan

Erie

Superior

The word "superior" means the biggest or the best. Lake Superior is the largest of the Great Lakes.

Bonus Review

A **detail** in a reading passage is a small part of the passage, just like one window in a building is a **detail** of the building.

Optional Prosody Exercise

Part F - Reading Aloud

Directions: Listen to your teacher read the sentences below. If your teacher calls on you to read one of the sentences, try to read it so that it sounds like someone speaking. Take your time. You can read the sentence silently before reading it aloud.

1. New Brunswick borders which American state?

2. All of Lake Michigan is in the United States.

3. You might be able to **infer** the answer, though, by looking at the names of the lakes and then taking a guess.

Lesson 8

Part A- Vocabulary: Words in Context

Directions: Choose the best word to fill in the blank for each sentence.

1. Because e-mail is so _____, some people say that writing letters is becoming a lost art.

    a. expensive

    b. popular

    c. new

2. My favorite time of year in the northeast is fall because that is when the _____ change color.

    a. seasons

    b. leaves

    c. clothes

3. We had a speaker come to our school to talk about nutrition. All the kids in the whole school had to squeeze into the _____ to listen to her.

    a. car

    b. costumes

    c. gym

Part B - Asking Questions

Directions: Read the short passage below. Write one question after each sentence in the passage. Your teacher will call on some students to read their questions and others to answer them.

The Great Lakes are all connected to each other.

_____

_____

Lake Superior is the biggest fresh water lake in the world. It is joined to Lake Huron by the St. Mary's river.

_____

_____

Lake Huron gets its water from Lake Michigan. The water comes through the Straits of Mackinac.

_____

_____

Lake Erie gets water from Lake Huron. The water comes through the Saint Clair River, Lake Saint Clair, and the Detroit River.

_____

_____

Lake Erie empties into Lake Ontario through the Niagara River.

_____

_____

Lake Ontario runs into the St. Lawrence River.

_____

_____

Part C- Inference Questions

Directions: Read the short passage below. Read each question and then read the hint that follows it. Finally, answer the inference question. The exact answer to the inference question is not in the passage.

William Penn was born in England in 1644. When he was 22 years old, he became a Quaker. Quakers didn't share the religious beliefs of the government. They were treated very badly. Many of them were arrested. William Penn was arrested many times. Penn wanted to create a place where people would be free to believe whatever they chose. In 1681 Penn got his chance. The king of England gave him an area of land in the New World. William Penn named the area Sylvania. That means "woods" in Latin. The king added "Penn" in honor of William's father. And so the area became known as Pennsylvania.

1. Why would William Penn become a Quaker?
    Hint: Maybe William Penn didn't share the religious beliefs of the government.

_____

_____

2. Why would the King want to honor William's father?
    Hint: Maybe William's father was a friend of the king. Maybe William's father did a lot for England.

_____

_____

3. Why would William name the area "woods" in Latin?

   Hint: Maybe there were many trees in the area.

_____

4. Why would the government want to arrest Quakers?

   Hint: Maybe the government thought arresting Quakers would stop people from becoming QUakers.

_____

Part D - Memory Techniques

Directions: Look at the chart of the Great Lakes below. This chart can help you remember some of the facts from Part B. It shows that both Lake Superior and Lake Michigan drain into Lake Huron, for example.

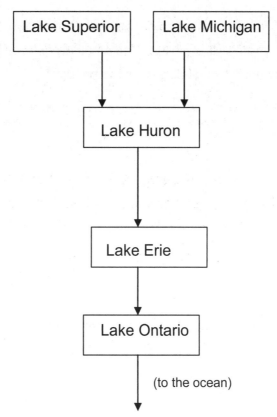

Also remember that if you can think of "HOMES," that will help you remember the names of the Great Lakes.

Huron
Ontario
Michigan
Erie
Superior

Part E- Bonus

Remember, **inference** means "guessing about something from another thing that you already know." When you read, you often have to **infer** something that isn't told to you directly in the passage.

To learn **inference,** you will have to know what it means, how to spell it, and where it comes from.

Bonus Review

A **detail** in a reading passage is a small part of the passage. In Part C, you read a passage about William Penn. The whole passage was about William Penn. One small **detail** from the passage is that William Penn was a Quaker. There are several small **details** in the passage.

Part F - Reading Aloud

Directions: Listen to your teacher read the sentences below. If your teacher calls on you to read one of the sentences, try to read it so that it sounds like someone speaking. Take your time. You can read the sentence silently before reading it aloud.

1. It shows that both Lake Superior and Lake Michigan drain into Lake Huron, for example.

2. Why would William name the area "woods" in Latin?

3. Because e-mail is so popular, some people say that writing letters is becoming a lost art.

Lesson 9

Part A- Vocabulary: Words in Context

Directions: Choose the word that would best fill in the blank in each sentence.

1. Every Friday, we all get to have a pizza party at school if our _____ class has behaved for the whole week.

   a. first

   b. entire

   c. big

2. When my sister and I go _____, I usually ask her to put the bait on the hook for me. I think worms are gross.

   a. hunting

   b. fishing

   c. swimming

3. Even though she is only three years old, my dog is so _____ that she sleeps all day.

   a. big

   b. lonely

   c. lazy

Part B- Inference Questions

Directions: Read the short passage below. Read each question and then read the hint that follows it. Finally, answer the inference question. The exact answer to the inference question is not in the passage.

Mark didn't know what to do. He was about to start college and he didn't know what to study. He loved computers. He'd worked with them almost his whole life. He knew all about computers. He also enjoyed making people feel better. His best friend was going to study computers. But he knew and loved the nursing teachers at his school. Finally, Mark chose to study nursing.

Lesson 9

1. Give *two* reasons why Mark might want to study computers.

   Hint: If you love something, you usually want to learn more about it. Studying with friends can be fun.

   _____

   _____

   _____

2. Give *two* reasons why Mark might want to study nursing.

   Hint: Good teachers can teach you a lot.

   _____

   _____

   _____

3. Why might Mark have finally decided to study nursing?

   Hint: Sometimes, it can be fun to do something different.

   _____

   _____

   _____

Part C- Reviewing Details

Directions: Follow your teacher's instructions.

There will be questions about Canada on the Lesson 10 Quiz.

1. Name the province of Canada that is furthest west.

   _____

2. Which province is **NOT** a maritime province?

   a. New Brunswick

   b. British Columbia

   c. P.E.I.

   d. Nova Scotia

3. What is the *2nd* largest country in the world?

   _____

4. What is the largest country in the world?

   _____

5. The population of Canada is about:

   a. 32,000

   b. 320,000

   c. 3,200,000

   d. 32,000,000

6. Name the *two* Canadian provinces that are furthest west.

   _____

7. Nova Scotia is a peninsula. The Latin word "insula" is related to what English word?

   _____

8. Which Canadian province borders the U.S. state of Maine?

_____

9. Which is the smallest Canadian province?

_____

10. How many Canadian provinces are there?

_____

Part D- Memory Techniques

Directions: Look at the map below, and then answer the questions about Canada.

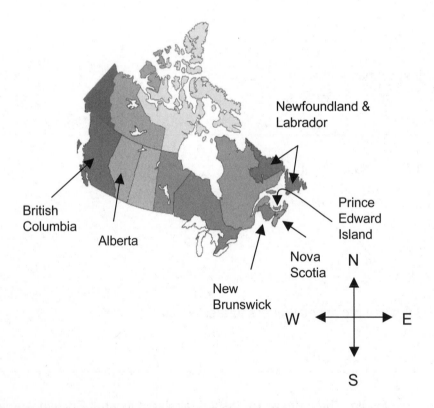

1. Which Canadian province is just east of British Columbia?

_____

2. Nova Scotia is a peninsula that connects to:

    a.   British Columbia

    b.   New Brunswick

    c.   Newfoundland and Labrador

    d.   Prince Edward Island

3. Name three provinces that are very small.

_____

4. Newfoundland and Labrador don't actually touch one another because Newfoundland is an island. Why do you think they are considered to be one province?

    Hint: Look carefully at the map.

_____

Part E- Bonus

Remember, **inference** means "guessing about something from another thing that you already know." When you read, you often have to **infer** something that isn't told to you directly in the passage.

To learn **inference,** you will have to know what it means, how to spell it, and where it comes from.

Bonus Review

A **detail** in a reading passage is a small part of the passage. In Part B, you read a passage about a decision Carol had to make. The whole passage was about Carol's decision. One small **detail** from the passage is that Carol's friend wanted Carol to switch from baseball to softball. There are several small **details** in the passage.

Optional Prosody Exercise

Part F - Reading Aloud

Directions: Listen to your teacher read the sentences below. If your teacher calls on you to read one of the sentences, try to read it so that it sounds like someone speaking.

1. To learn **inference**, you will have to know what it means, how to spell it, and where it comes from.

2. But he knew and loved the nursing teachers at his school.

3. The Latin word "insula" is related to what English word?

Lesson 10

Optional Prosody Exercise

Part C - Reading Aloud

Directions: Listen to your teacher read the sentences below. If your teacher calls on you to read one of the sentences, try to read it so that it sounds like someone speaking.

1. What language do **MOST** people in Canada speak?

2. Instead of having lungs, fish breathe through *gills*.

3. What is a fish scale like?

Lesson 11

Part A - Words in Context

Directions: After you read each model, choose the word from the list below that could *best* replace the underlined word in the model.

HINT: The words in bold type are a clue about the missing word.

1. **Model:** The new **shopping** center in our town is wonderful. You can <u>purchase</u> just about anything there **if you have the money**.

   a. see

   b. find

   c. buy

   d. sell

2. **Model:** Lenore has all her **favorite** <u>possessions</u> in her bedroom. She keeps them **in a safe** that she got as a birthday present.

    a.   things

    b.   snacks

    c.   books

    d.   pets

3. **Model:** Mrs. O'Conner next door has a large vegetable garden. Instead of being shaped like a rectangle, it is <u>circular</u>. She has a bird bath **in the center**, with rows of flowers **coming out like spokes on a wheel**.

    a.   flat

    b.   open

    c.   square

    d.   round

Part B - Vocabulary

Directions: Read the definitions below. Fill in the blank in each definition with the word from the list that best fits the sentence. Try to do this without looking at Part A.

possessions

purchase

circular

1. _____ are the things you own. Some of those things are very important to you. Some are not as important.

2. When you make a _____, you buy something. You might purchase one item, or several.

3. _____ means round. A circular saw is a power saw with a round saw blade.

Part C - Asking Questions

Directions: Read the short passage below. Write one question after each sentence in the passage. Your teacher will call on some students to read their questions and others to answer them.

The largest province in Canada is Québec.

_____

_____

The first permanent French settlement in North America was in Québec.

_____

_____

It is not surprising, then, that the majority of people in Québec speak French as their first language.

_____

_____

Therefore, both English and French are official languages in Canada.

_____

_____

Products in grocery stores throughout Canada, for example, have both French and English labels.

_____

_____

In French, Québec is pronounced like this: kay BECK.

_____

_____

Part D- Memory Techniques

Write the names of the provinces next to the correct arrows on the map below. Remember, the *largest* province in Canada is Québec.

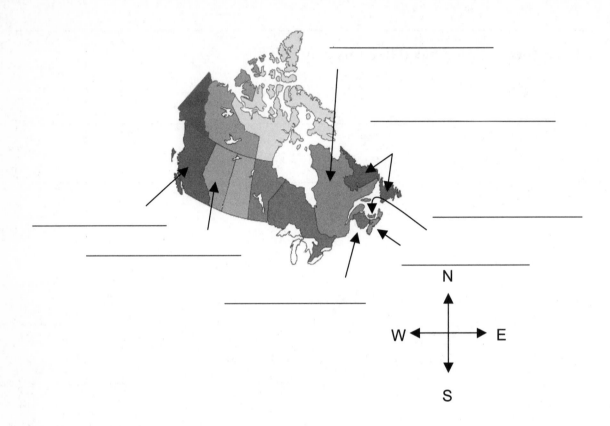

Part E- Bonus

Every well-written paragraph or passage is *mostly about* one thing. You have read passages that are *mostly about* Canada, *mostly about* The Great Lakes, and *mostly about* classes of animals.

Here is a paragraph that is *mostly about* reptiles:

Snakes, turtles, and lizards are reptiles. Like fish, reptiles hatch from eggs. They usually have dry skin that is thick, and often they have scales. Reptiles are cold-blooded. That means that the temperature around them changes the temperature of their bodies. Reptiles breathe through their lungs, just as mammals do.

There is no sentence in the paragraph that says something like, "This paragraph is mostly about reptiles." You can tell what the paragraph is about because all the **details** are about reptiles.

Optional Prosody Exercise

Part F - Reading Aloud

Directions: Listen to your teacher read the sentences below. If your teacher calls on you to read one of the sentences, try to read it so that it sounds like someone speaking.

1. Every well-written paragraph or passage is *mostly about* one thing.

2. A circular saw is a power saw with a round saw blade.

3. Possessions are the things you own.

Lesson 12

Part A - Words in Context

Directions: After you read each model, choose the word from the list below that could *best* replace the underlined word in the model sentence.

HINT: The words in bold type are a clue about the missing word.

1. **Model:** There was the <u>scent</u> of baking cookies coming from Mark's kitchen. **His nose told him** that the cookies were **chocolate chip** and that they were **almost done**.

    a. smell

    b. look

    c. feel

    d. sense

2. **Model**: Mary ran a mile in less than 7 minutes on her first <u>attempt</u>. She had **never done that before** and was very happy.

    a.   team

    b.   try

    c.   day

    d.   track

3. **Model:** Jane is <u>intelligent</u>. She **does very well in school** and always has a lot to talk about.

    a.   silly

    b.   sad

    c.   smart

    d.   funny

Part B - Vocabulary

Directions: Read the definitions below. Fill in the blank in each definition with the word from the list that best fits the sentence. Try to do this without looking at Part A.

scent

attempt

intelligent

1. The _____ of baking cookies is the smell of baking cookies. Scents can tell you a lot, like the kind of cookie that is baking, and if those cookies are burning.

2. Another word for _____ is try. If you attempt to make your dreams come true, you try to make your dreams come true.

3. _____ means smart. People can be intelligent and so can animals.

Part C- Reviewing Details

Directions: Follow your teacher's instructions.

1. Name the province of Canada that is next to British Columbia.

2. What is the largest province in Canada?

    a.   British Columbia

    b.   Québec

    c.   Newfoundland & Labrador

    d.   Alberta

3. What English word is related to the Latin word, *insula*?

_____

4. Which Canadian province is a peninsula?

_____

5. The population of Canada is about:

_____

6. Name the smallest Canadian province.

_____

7. In Québec, the first language of most people is:

_____

8. Which Canadian province shares a border with the state of Maine?

_____

9. What is the 2nd largest country in the world?

_____

10. The word "superior" in Lake Superior hints that Lake Superior is the _____ Great Lake.

    a.   coldest

    b.   smallest

    c.   largest

    d.   most blue

Part D - Memory Techniques

Directions: This chart shows that two lakes flow into Lake Huron. Write the name of the missing Great Lake.

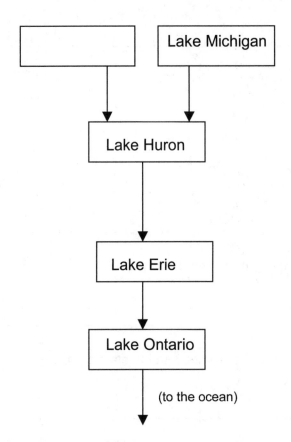

Also remember that if you can think of "HOMES," that will help you remember the names of the Great Lakes.

Part E - Inference

Directions: Read the passage below. Think about how the characters *feel* in the passage, and then answer the questions below.

Tara's parents got her a puppy for her birthday. The puppy had golden fur. Tara named her Marigold. Tara woke up early every morning to take Marigold for a walk. She always shared her after school snack with Marigold. And Marigold slept at the foot of Tara's bed every night. One day, Marigold wasn't there when Tara got home from school. Marigold had gotten out of the yard! Tara cried and cried. Then the doorbell rang. Tara's mom answered the door and there was Marigold! Another family found her. They brought her home. Tara gave Marigold a big kiss right on the nose.

1. How did Tara probably feel when she first got Marigold?

    a. scared

    b. excited

    c. angry

    d. nervous

2. When Tara's mom saw Tara taking such good care of Marigold, Tara's mom probably thought that Tara:

    a. didn't like Marigold

    b. was lazy

    c. was too young for a puppy

    d. was very responsible

3. How did Tara probably feel when she found out Marigold was missing?

    a. sad

    b. happy

    c. relieved

    d. excited

4. How did Tara probably feel when Marigold came home?

    a. angry

    b. thrilled

    c. unhappy

    d. bored

Part F- Bonus

Every well-written paragraph or passage is **mostly about** one thing. The **details** show you what the paragraph or passage is **mostly about.** For example, a paragraph that is **mostly about** mammals has a lot of **details** about mammals.

Optional Prosody Exercise

Part G- Reading Aloud

Directions: Listen to your teacher read the sentences below. If your teacher calls on you to read one of the sentences, try to read it so that it sounds like someone speaking.

1. Tara's mom answered the door and there was Marigold!

2. Which Canadian province is a peninsula?

3. She does very well in school and always has a lot to talk about.

Lesson 13

Part A - Words in Context

Directions: After you read each model, choose the word from the list below that could *best* **replace the underlined word in the model sentence.**

HINT: The words in bold type are a clue about the missing word.

1. **Model:** Peter had to read a <u>brief</u> story for homework. It **only took him ten minutes** to finish reading it.

    a.   long

    b.   funny

    c.   scary

    d.   short

2. **Model:** My mother **ironed** my skirt five times to get the <u>creases</u> out. She wanted it to be **flat and smooth** for my first day of school.

    a.   folds

    b.   lines

    c.   dirt

    d.   color

3. **Model:** My father and I will **dig** a <u>ditch</u> so we can **plant** a row of roses. It doesn't have to be very wide, but it does have to be **deep**.

    a.   long hole

    b.   row

    c.   lot

    d.   square

Part B - Vocabulary

Directions: Read the definitions below. Fill in the blank in each definition with the word from the list that best fits the sentence. Try to do this without looking at Part A.

attempt

brief

possessions

circular

creases

ditch

1.   Short is another word for _____. If you had a short wait at the bakery, you could say you had a brief wait.

2. _____ are folds. One way to get creases out of clothing is to iron them.

3. A word for a long hole is _____. You can dig a ditch with a shovel or with your hands.

4. _____ means round. The earth is circular.

5. Another word for _____ is try. If you try to make an apple pie, you attempt to make an apple pie.

6. _____ are the things you own. Some of your important possessions may be your diary or your favorite baseball card.

Part C- Reviewing Details

Directions: Follow your teacher's instructions.

1. New Brunswick borders which American state?

_____

2. What is the largest province in Canada?

    a. British Columbia

    b. Québec

    c. Newfoundland & Labrador

    d. Alberta

3. What is the smallest province in Canada?

    a. New Brunswick

    b. Nova Scotia

    c. P.E.I

    d. British Columbia

4. Which Canadian province is an island?

_____

5. The population of Canada is about:

    a. 3,200,000

    b. the same as California

    c. the same as Maine

    d. the same as Russia

6. In Québec, the first language of most people is:

_____

7. Which Canadian province shares a border with the state of Maine?

    a. New Brunswick

    b. British Columbia

    c. Alberta

8. What is the largest country in the world?

_____

9. Outside of Québec, most Canadians speak:

_____

Part D - Memory Techniques

Directions: Read the paragraph below. Next, answer the questions.

You know that there are five lakes in North America that are called the **Great Lakes**. Lake Michigan is the only one that lies completely inside the United States. The other four are all partly in the northern part of the United States. The lakes are all connected to one another. Lake Superior is the largest of the five lakes. That is why it is called "superior." The chart below shows that Lake Superior and Lake Michigan flow into Lake Huron.

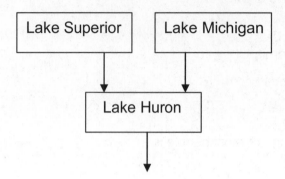

1. Lake Huron receives water from which other two Great Lakes?

_____

2. Four of the lakes are partly in the northern part of the United States. What other country must border them?

_____

3. Which Great Lake is the largest?

_____

4. What word helps you remember the names of the Great Lakes?

_____

5. The lake furthest to the west is shown in the upper left box of the chart. Which lake is that?

_____

6. Water from Lake Michigan flows into which lake?

_____

Part E- Bonus

Every well-written paragraph or passage is **mostly about** one thing. The **details** show you what the paragraph or passage is **mostly about.**

The passage in Part D is **mostly about** The Great Lakes. One **detail** about The Great Lakes is that Lake Superior and Lake Michigan both flow into Lake Huron.

Optional Prosody Exercise

Part F- Reading Aloud

Directions: Your teacher is *not* going to read the sentences below. If your teacher calls on you to read one of the sentences, try to read it so that it sounds like someone speaking.

1. My mother ironed my skirt five times to get the creases out.

2. What word helps you remember the names of the Great Lakes?

3. One **detail** about The Great Lakes is that Lake Superior and Lake Michigan both flow into Lake Huron.

Lesson 14

Part A - Words in Context

Directions: After you read each model, choose the word from the list below that could *best* replace the underlined word in the model sentence.

HINT: The words in bold type are a clue about the missing word.

1. **Model:** Jody was looking for a <u>flesh</u> colored crayon to finish her picture of her mother. She used a brown one for her mother's **eyes and hair**, but she needed one for her **face.**

    a. skin

    b. green

    c. shoe

    d. wall

2. **Model:** The sheep **got through** a <u>gap</u> in the fence. It was **only wide enough** for one sheep to go through at a time.

    a. line

    b. circle

    c. square

    d. space

Part B- Vocabulary

Directions: Read the definitions below. Fill in the blank in each definition with the word from the list that best fits the sentence. Try to do this without looking at Part A.

    purchase

    flesh

    scent

    gap

    crease

    brief

1. _____ is another way of saying smell. Every perfume has its own scent or smell.

2. Another word for buy is _____. Another way of saying, "Buy one, get one free," is, "Purchase one, get one free."

3. One meaning of _____ is skin. If a cat scratched your flesh, you could also say it scratched your skin.

4. Short is another word for _____. If you make a brief speech, you make a short speech.

5. _____ means space. Sometimes there is a gap in something, like a fence. Sometimes there is a gap between two things, like a car and the sidewalk.

6. To _____ is to fold. You can make creases in paper to make a paper airplane.

Part C- Remembering What You Read

Directions: Answer the questions about Canada below.

1. The maritime provinces of Canada are Nova Scotia, P.E.I., and:

    _____

2. The largest Canadian province is what?

    a. British Columbia

    b. Québec

    c. Alberta

3. What are the two official languages spoken in Canada?

    a. English and French

    b. French and Canadian

    c. English and Canadian

    d. French and Scottish

4. What English word is related to the Latin word *insula*?

    _____

5. Which Canadian province is a peninsula?

    _____

6. Which Canadian province is an island?

    _____

Part D- Memory Techniques

Directions: Answer the literal questions. Refer to the map below.

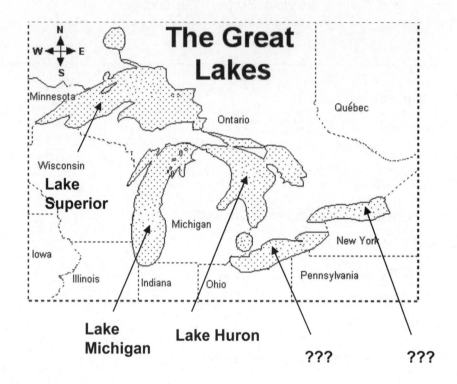

1. Lake Huron receives water from which other two Great Lakes?

_____

2. Which lake is mostly bordered by Wisconsin on the west side and Michigan on the east side?

_____

3. Which Great Lake is the largest?

_____

4. What word helps you remember the names of the Great Lakes?

_____

5. Which two lakes are not labeled on this map?

_____

6. Which lake is furthest to the west?

_____

7. Water from Lake Superior flows into which lake?

_____

Part E- Bonus

Every well-written paragraph or passage is *mostly about* one thing. You have read passages that are *mostly about* Canada, *mostly about* The Great Lakes, and *mostly about* classes of animals.

Here is a paragraph you've read before. It is *mostly about* fish:

Fish are a *class* of *vertebrates*. Fish are *aquatic*. That means they live in water, as you know. Instead of having lungs, fish breathe through *gills*. Fish get oxygen out of the water that passes through their gills. Most fish hatch out of eggs, and most fish have *scales*. Each scale is flat, small, and hard. The scales overlap each other like the shingles on a roof. The scales help protect the fish.

There is no sentence in the paragraph that says something like, "This paragraph is mostly about fish." You can tell what the paragraph is about because all the **details** are about fish.

Optional Prosody Exercise

Part F- Reading Aloud

Directions: Your teacher is *not* going to read the sentences below. If your teacher calls on you to read one of the sentences, try to read it so that it sounds like someone speaking.

1. It was only wide enough for one sheep to go through at a time.

2. Water from Lake Superior flows into which lake?

3. Sometimes there is a gap in something, like a fence.

Lesson 15

Optional Prosody Exercise

Part C- Reading Aloud

Directions: Your teacher is *not* going to read the sentences below. If your teacher calls on you to read one of the sentences, try to read it so that it sounds like someone speaking.

1. What language is spoken by most people in the largest Canadian province?

2. That means that the temperature around them changes the temperature of their bodies.

3. What do reptiles and mammals have in common?

Lesson 16

Part A - Words in Context

Directions: After you read each model, choose the word from the list below that could *best* replace the underlined word in the model sentence.

HINT: The words in bold type are a clue about the missing word.

1. **Model:** The bang of the fireworks was <u>deafening</u>. My little sister **covered her ears** when she heard it.

   a. very quiet

   b. like music

   c. very loud

   d. very funny

2. **Model:** Jen <u>injured</u> her knee playing soccer. She **had to go to the doctor** after practice.

    a. hurt

    b. helped

    c. saved

    d. pulled

Part B - Vocabulary

Directions: Read the definitions below. Fill in the blank in each definition with the word from the list that best fits the sentence.

    deafening

    injured

    ditches

    attempt

    flesh

    intelligent

1. Something that is very loud is called _____. Music and fireworks are two things that can be deafening.

2. _____ are long holes. Cars can sometimes get stuck in ditches.

3. Another way of saying _____ is smart. Studying for tests is the intelligent thing to do.

4. _____ means hurt. People try not to get injured.

5. Another word for try is _____. People should always attempt to do their best.

6. _____ can mean skin. Flesh can be a lot of different colors.

Part C - Asking Questions

Directions: Read the short passage below. Write one question after each sentence in the passage. Your teacher will call on some students to read their questions and others to answer them.

The province in Canada that goes the furthest south is Ontario.

_____

_____

Ontario is the second largest Canadian province, after Québec.

_____

_____

Ontario, however, has the largest _population_ of any Canadian province.

_____

_____

The capital of Canada is the city of Ottawa, Ontario.

_____

_____

The largest city in Canada is also in Ontario: the city of Toronto.

_____

_____

Part D- Memory Techniques

Directions: Answer the literal questions. Refer to the map below.

1. Lake Huron flows into a smaller lake, and then into which Great Lake?
    Hint: Look for the smaller Great Lake right below Lake Huron.

_____

2. The name of which lake is missing on this map?

_____

3. Which Great Lake is the smallest?

_____

4. Which lake is furthest to the east?

_____

Part E- Bonus

Fiction is a type of writing created from the imagination of the writer. Fiction is not from history or fact. Although people write stories that are based on history or true experiences, most *stories* are fiction. Many times, you can tell immediately that a story is fiction because there are things in the story that couldn't be true, such as talking animals. Sometimes, a fictional story seems very real, but it comes from an author's imagination, nonetheless.

Fict comes from a Latin word that means: shaping or molding. Authors of **fiction** "shape" or "mold" a story from their imaginations.

Fiction will be a bonus item on some quizzes or tests that you take. To learn **fiction,** you will have to know what it means, how to spell it, and where it comes from.

Bonus Review

Remember, a **detail** in a reading passage is a small part of the passage. The word **detail** comes from a Latin word that means "cut."

When you read, you often have to **infer** something that isn't told to you directly in the passage.

Inference comes from Latin.

Optional Prosody Exercise

Part F- Reading Aloud

Directions: If your teacher calls on you to read one of the sentences, try to read it so that it sounds like someone speaking.

1. Fiction is a type of writing created from the imagination of the writer.

2. Studying for tests is the intelligent thing to do.

Lesson 17

Part A - Words in Context

Directions: After you read each model, choose the word from the list below that could *best* replace the underlined word in the model sentence. Then, list one or two words from the model that helped you figure out the meaning of the underlined word.

1. **Model:** The loud sound of my older sister's music really <u>irritates</u> me when I'm trying to study.

    a. soothes

    b. bothers

    c. excites

    d. pleases

2. **Model:** Don't <u>omit</u> the table of contents from your report. All the parts need to be there.

    a. leave out

    b. include

    c. put

    d. type

Part B - Mostly About

Directions: Read the passage below, which is mostly about the string family of musical instruments in an orchestra, and then follow the directions.

An orchestra has "families" of instruments. One family is called "strings." You can tell by the name that all the instruments in this family have strings. For example, a violin is an instrument in the strings family. A cello (CHELL oh) is also in the strings family. A harp is in the strings family too. Although a piano has strings, it is usually not considered part of the string family.

Put an X next to each statement that is a small *detail* from the passage about the string family of instruments. Four of the statements are details from the passage. Don't write anything next to the one statement that is not a detail from the passage.

1. _____ "Strings" is a family of instruments in an orchestra.
2. _____ Orchestras have many instruments.
3. _____ Violins are in the strings family.
4. _____ Pianos are not in the strings family.
5. _____ A member of the strings family is the harp.

Part C- Memory Techniques

Directions: Answer the literal questions. Refer to the map below.

1. Which two lakes flow into Lake Huron?

2. The name of which lake is missing on this map?

_____

3. Which Great Lake is the largest?

_____

4. Which lake is furthest to the west?

_____

5. Which lake goes the furthest east?

_____

Part D- Review

Directions: Read the passage, and then answer the questions.

Marcia couldn't wait for soccer season to start. She had been practicing her skills and she had gotten to be much better than the year before. She wanted her teammates to see how well she could play.

1. Which word best describes how Marcia felt about the new soccer season?

    a.   eager

    b.   afraid

    c.   interested

2. What had Marcia been practicing?

    a.   the piano

    b.   kicking

    c.   skills

3. When her teammates see Marcia play, they will probably be:

    a. tired

    b. at home

    c. surprised

4. Write one question about this passage.

_____

_____

Part E- Bonus

Fiction is a type of writing created from the imagination of the writer, not from history or fact.

Fict comes from a Latin word that means: shaping or molding. Authors of **fiction** "shape" or "mold" a story from their imaginations.

Fiction will be a bonus item on some quizzes or tests that you take.

Bonus Review

Remember, every well-written paragraph or passage is ***mostly about*** one thing. The paragraph or passage gives **details** of that one thing.

Inference means "guessing about something from another thing that you already know." When you read, you often have to **infer** something that isn't told to you directly in the passage.

Inference comes from Latin.

Optional Prosody Exercise

Part F- Reading Aloud

Directions: If your teacher calls on you to read one of the sentences, try to read it so that it sounds like someone speaking.

1. She had been practicing her skills and she had gotten to be much better than the year before.

2. Although a piano has strings, it is not usually considered part of the string family.

Lesson 18

Part A - Vocabulary

Directions: Read the definitions below. Fill in the blank in each definition with the word from the list that best fits the sentence.

omit

injured

irritates

creases

possessions

1. The things you own are your _____.

2. You can _____ your middle initial on this form. It isn't necessary.

3. Makail got hit in the head with a softball during recess, but he's not _____ badly. He just has a little bump on his head.

4. I stuffed my report into my backpack and it came out with _____ all over it. My backpack was too full, I guess.

5. When you scratch your fingernails on a chalkboard, the sound really _____ a lot of people.

Part B - Mostly About

Directions: Read the passage below, which is mostly about the percussion family of musical instruments in an orchestra, and then follow the directions.

In Lesson 17 you read about instruments called "strings." "Percussion" is the name of another family of instruments. Percussion instruments are also found in an orchestra. Most percussion instruments make sounds when you hit them. Drums are in the percussion family. Bells are also percussion instruments. Cymbals are big metal circles that you bang together to make a sound. They are also part of the percussion family of instruments.

Put an X next to each statement that is a small *detail* from the passage about the percussion family of instruments. Four of the statements are details from the passage. Don't write anything next to the one statement that is not a detail from the passage.

1. _____ You can bang on things or hit them to make sound.
2. _____ Drums are percussion instruments.
3. _____ Cymbals are made of metal.
4. _____ Bells are in the percussion family.
5. _____ Cymbals are banged together.

Part C- Remembering What You Read

Directions: Answer the questions about Canada below.

1. What is the second largest province in Canada?

    a. Ontario

    b. Québec

    c. Nova Scotia

    d. Newfoundland & Labrador

2. The largest Canadian province is what?

    a. British Columbia

    b. Québec

    c. Alberta

    d. Ontario

3. Ottawa is the capital city of what country?

    _____

4. What English word is related to the Latin word *insula*?

    _____

5. What is the largest city in Canada?

    a. Toronto

    b. Ottawa

    c. Alberta

6. Which Canadian province is an island?

_____

7. The largest city in Canada is located in which province?

_____

Part D- Memory Techniques

Directions: Write the names of the provinces next to the correct arrows on the map below. Some of the province names are already written for you.

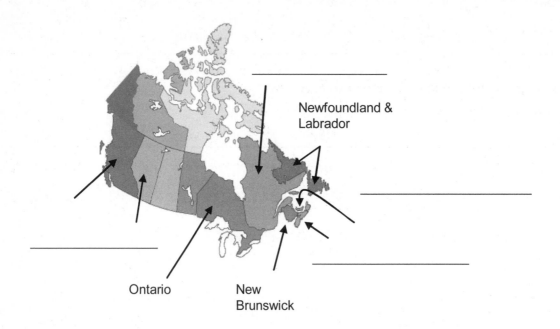

Newfoundland & Labrador

Ontario

New Brunswick

Part E- Bonus

Fiction is a type of writing created from the imagination of the writer, rather than from history or fact. Most stories are fiction. The author makes up the characters and events in the story. The reason authors write fiction, usually, is to entertain the reader.

Bonus Review

Remember, every well-written paragraph or passage is ***mostly about*** one thing. The paragraph or passage gives **details** of that one thing.

Inference means "guessing about something from another thing that you already know."

Optional Prosody Exercise

Part F- Reading Aloud

Directions: If your teacher calls on you to read one of the sentences, try to read it so that it sounds like someone speaking.

1. The reason authors write fiction, usually, is to entertain the reader.

2. Makail got hit in the head with a softball during recess, but he's not injured badly.

Lesson 19

Part A - Words in Context

Directions: Read the definitions below. Fill in the blank in each definition with the word from the list that best fits the sentence. List one or two words from the model that helped you figure out the meaning of each underlined word.

1. **Model:** The <u>author</u> of that book did a great job. He wrote it to be fun and easy to read.

    a. reader

    b. singer

    c. writer

    d. seller

2. **Model:** My school's <u>banner</u> looks great flying from its pole in the wind. You can see all of our school colors.

    a. flag

    b. window

    c. shirt

    d. balloon

Part B - Mostly About

Directions: Read the passage below, which is mostly about the brass family of musical instruments in an orchestra, and then follow the directions.

"Brass" is the name of another group of instruments. Brass instruments are also part of an orchestra. The instruments in the brass family are made of brass or some other metal. The musicians make a "raspberry" kind of sound in the mouthpiece of brass instruments. The sound goes through the instrument and makes musical sounds. Trumpets are one kind of brass instruments. Tubas and trombones are also brass instruments.

Put an X next to each statement that is a small *detail* from the passage about the brass family of instruments. Four of the statements are details from the passage. Don't write anything next to the one statement that is not a detail from the passage.

1. _____ Brass instruments are made of metal.
2. _____ One type of brass instrument is the trumpet.
3. _____ Some musical instruments have a mouthpiece.
4. _____ Trombones are in the brass family.
5. _____ Tubas are in the brass family.

Part C- Reviewing Details

Directions: Follow your teacher's instructions.

1. What is the capital city of Canada?

   _____

2. What is the largest Great Lake?

   _____

3. What is the largest province in Canada?

   _____

4. What is the largest city in Canada?

   _____

5. What is the smallest Great Lake:

   a.   Lake Superior

   b.   Lake Ontario

6. What does Nova Scotia mean?

   _____

7. What memory device helps you remember the names of the Great Lakes?

   _____

8. Which Canadian province is furthest west?

   _____

9. How many provinces does Canada have?

_____

10. What is the largest country in the world?

_____

Part D- Memory Techniques

Directions: Answer the literal questions. Refer to the map below.

1. The names of which two lakes are missing on this map?

_____

2. Which two lakes flow into Lake Huron?

_____

3. Which Great Lake is the smallest?

_____

4. Which lake is furthest to the east?

_____

5. Which lake goes the furthest west?

_____

Part E- Bonus

Fiction is a type of writing created from the imagination of the writer, not from history or fact. The author makes up the characters and events in the story. Fictional stories are often entertaining.

Bonus Review

Every well-written paragraph or passage is ***mostly about*** one thing. The paragraph or passage gives **details** of that one thing.

Inference means "guessing about something from another thing that you already know." **Inference** comes from Latin.

Optional Prosody Exercise

Part F- Reading Aloud

Directions: If your teacher calls on you to read one of the sentences, try to read it so that it sounds like someone speaking.

1. What is the largest country in the world?

2. Fiction is a type of writing created from the imagination of the writer, not from history or fact.

Lesson 21

Part A - Vocabulary

Directions: Write the words from below that best fit the definitions.

author

banner

irritates

omit

circular

1. I want to buy the _____ of my favorite baseball team. I can't fly it from a pole, but I can hang it up in my room.

2. It really _____ me when it rains and I can't play baseball.

3. For years people thought the Earth was flat, but then they found out it is _____.

4. I love writing stories, so I was thinking of becoming an _____ when I grow up.

5. I have trouble spelling, so I always double check my writing to make sure I didn't _____ any letters.

Part B- Asking Questions

Directions: Read the short passage below. Write as many questions about the passage as you can think of. Your teacher will call on some students to read their questions and others to answer them.

You have read about eight Canadian provinces. They are: British Columbia, Alberta, Newfoundland and Labrador, Prince Edward Island, Nova Scotia, New Brunswick, Ontario, and Québec. Canada has ten provinces altogether. The other two provinces are Saskatchewan and Manitoba. Saskatchewan is pronounced "sas CATCH uh wan." It is directly east of Alberta. A lot of Saskatchewan is a large plain or prairie with rich soil. The soil makes Saskatchewan a perfect place to grow wheat.

Manitoba is east of Saskatchewan, next to Ontario. The southern part of Manitoba is a flat plain. Taken together, Saskatchewan, Manitoba, and Alberta are called the *prairie provinces*. The middle part of Manitoba has forests and thousands of lakes.

_____

_____

_____

_____

_____

_____

Part C - Mostly About

Directions: Read the passage below, which is mostly about the woodwind family of musical instruments in an orchestra. Next, answer the questions.

At one time, nearly all the instruments in the "woodwind" section in an orchestra were made of wood. The woodwind instruments are played by blowing air into them. The word "wind" means blowing air. That is how the woodwinds got their name: blowing air through a wooden instrument.

Today, woodwind instruments are made of a lot of materials. Flutes are made of metal. Other woodwind instruments include piccolos, clarinets, saxophones, oboes, and bassoons. To play the flute, the musician blows air over a hole. To play the clarinet or the saxophone, the musician blows air across a reed. A reed is a very thin piece of wood.

Put an X next to each statement that is a small *detail* from the passage about the woodwind family of instruments.

1. _____ Woodwinds used to be made of wood.
2. _____ There are many families of instruments in a band.
3. _____ A flute is a woodwind instrument.
4. _____ Clarinets have reeds.
5. _____ Woodwinds are now made of different materials.

Part D- Memory Techniques

Write the missing names of the provinces next to the correct arrows on the map below. Notice where Saskatchewan and Manitoba are. Select your answers from these names: Alberta, New Brunswick, Prince Edward Island, Québec and Nova Scotia.

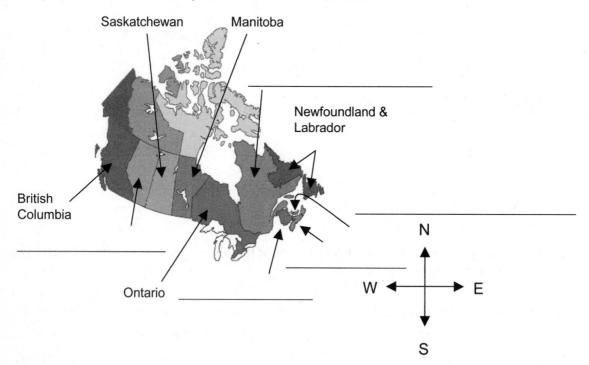

Part E - Bonus - Pronouns

The passage below is strange. Read it and then raise your hand when you think you know why it is strange.

Barbara loves baseball. Barbara is a great baseball player. Barbara's dad taught Barbara how to pitch. Barbara's mom taught Barbara how to hit. Barbara's parents practice with Barbara whenever they can. Everyone on Barbara's baseball team says Barbara is the best. Barbara also loves to watch baseball. Barbara likes watching baseball on TV. But Barbara really likes going to baseball games.

Below is a normal version of the same passage. Read that version.

Barbara loves baseball. **She** is a great baseball player. Barbara's dad taught **her** how to pitch. **Her** mom taught **her** how to hit. Barbara's parents practice with **her** whenever they can. Everyone on Barbara's baseball team says **she** is the best. Barbara also loves to watch baseball. **She** likes watching baseball on TV. But **she** really likes going to baseball games.

In the second passage, there are **pronouns** used to refer to Barbara. The **pronouns** are **her** and **she**.

Lesson 22

Part A - Vocabulary

Directions: After you read each model, choose the word from the list that could *best* replace the underlined word in the model sentence. List one or two words in the model that helped you figure out the meaning for each underlined word.

1. **Model:** Sue got a great <u>bargain</u> on her shoes! They were on sale and cost only $5.00.

    a. color

    b. deal

    c. number

    d. heel

    _____

2. **Model:** They knew the mummy they found was <u>ancient</u>, but they had to do tests on it to find out just how old it was.

    a. dirty

    b. new

    c. very old

    d. broken

    _____

Part B- Memory Techniques

Directions: Write the name of each Great Lake.

Hints: (1) think about "HOMES" (2) the name of the largest lake can mean "big" or "large" or "best" and (3) the name of one lake is the same as the state next to it.

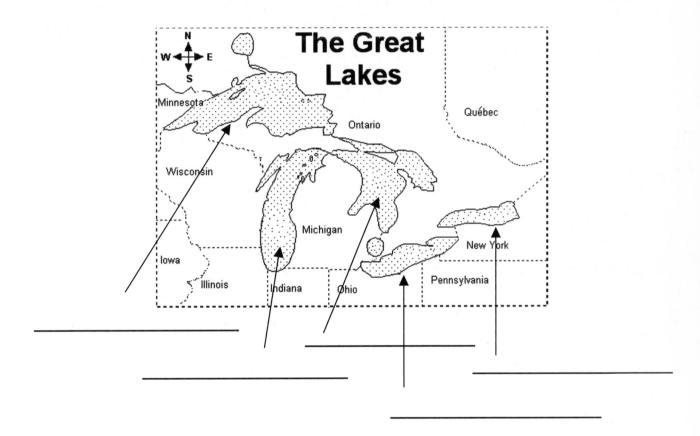

Part C- Reviewing Details

Directions: Follow your teacher's instructions.

1. What is the largest city in Canada?

_____

2. What is the smallest province in Canada?

_____

3. How many provinces does Canada have?

_____

4. Which Canadian province has two names?

    a.   British Columbia and Manitoba

    b.   Newfoundland and Labrador

    c.   Nova Scotia and New Brunswick

    d.   Prince Edward Island and Saskatchewan

5. What is the largest province in Canada?

_____

Part D- Review

Directions: Read the passage, and then answer the questions.

Missy is the greatest cat around. First, she is very friendly. If you call her name, she will go to you. Not too many cats come when they are called, so I think Missy is an <u>intelligent</u> cat. She loves to have you scratch her ears. Missy is also beautiful, and she has long, soft hair.

Even though Missy is pretty and friendly, she is also a good hunter. There are no moles or mice in our neighborhood. The only bad thing is that sometimes when Missy kills a mouse, she leaves it at someone's door.

1. According to the passage, do cats usually go to a person who is calling their name?

_____

2. Why are there no moles or mice in Missy's neighborhood?

_____

3. This is an **inference** question. The passage doesn't say, but who is probably telling this story?

    a.   just some person who likes cats

    b.   a dog and cat doctor

    c.   someone who lives in the same neighborhood as Missy

    d.   someone who doesn't like moles

4. This is another **inference** question. When the person telling the story sees a dead mouse, she probably feels:

    a.   grossed out

    b.   happy

    c.   irritated

    d.   sad

5. In this passage, <u>intelligent</u> means:

_____

6. Put an X next to each statement that is a small *detail* from the passage about Missy.

    1. _____ Missy is smart.

    2. _____ Missy is a good hunter.

    3. _____ Cats are intelligent.

    4. _____ Missy is a cat.

    5. _____ You can scratch Missy's ears.

Part E - Bonus - Pronouns

Here is the passage about Donna. The pronouns **she** and **her** refer to Donna. If you count the number of times Donna is referred to by her name, by **she**, and by **her**, that will tell you how many total times this short passage mentions Donna.

Donna loves to read about old airplanes. **She** also likes to build models of old airplanes. **Her** mom helps **her** with **her** models, especially with the painting. Donna enjoys working with **her** mom on airplane models. That's something that **she** and **her** mom can do together on a rainy day.

Donna: **2** + she: **2** + her: **5 = 9** times this passage mentions Donna

BONUS REVIEW

Inference means "guessing about something from another thing that you already know." When you read, you often have to **infer** something that isn't told to you directly in the passage.

Every well-written paragraph or passage is **mostly about** one thing. The passage above is **mostly about** Donna. The rest of the passage tells some **details** about Donna.

Fiction is a type of writing created from the imagination of the writer, rather than from history or fact.

Lesson 23

Part A - Vocabulary

Directions: Write the words from below that fit the definitions.

intelligent

banners

ancient

author

bargains

1. There are so many _____ in the world. Every country has one and so do many states, cities, and towns.

2. There is an _____ book in the museum which is under glass to protect it.

3. Jane thinks very hard about every decision she makes. She wants to make _____ choices.

4. I can't wait until my favorite _____ comes out with her new book.

5. I'm trying to save money, so whenever I go shopping, I look for good _____.

Part B- Memory Techniques

You have studied the names of the ten provinces in Canada, but if you don't live in Canada, it can be hard to remember those names. Here is a way to help remember the names of all ten provinces, from west to east.

Do a little chant that goes like this:

B - A - S (pause)

M - O - Q (pause)

3 N's and a P.E.I.

This stands for:

British Columbia, **A**lberta, **S**askatchewan

Manitoba, **O**ntario, **Q**uébec

New Brunswick, **N**ova Scotia, **N**ewfoundland & Labrador, and **P**rince **E**dward **I**sland

Practice this chant now, following your teacher's directions.

Part C- Remembering What You Read

Directions: Answer the questions about Canada below.

1. What is the largest city in Canada?

    a. Toronto

    b. Ottawa

    c. Saskatchewan

2. The largest Canadian province is what?

    a. British Columbia

    b. Québec

    c. Alberta

    d. Ontario

3. What is the capital city of Canada?

    a. Toronto

    b. Ottawa

    c. Saskatchewan

4. The English word "island" is related to which Latin word?

    a. prima

    b. scotia

    c. insula

    d. nova

5. The province of Saskatchewan is bordered by Manitoba on the east and _____ on the west.

    a. Alberta

    b. British Columbia

    c. Ontario

    d. Québec

6. Which Canadian province is an island?

_____

7. The "prairie provinces" are Saskatchewan, Alberta, and what?

    a. British Columbia

    b. Manitoba

    c. New Brunswick

    d. Ontario

Part D- Review

Directions: Read the passage, and then answer the questions.

"You're a Grand Old Flag" is a very <u>famous</u> song. It's about the US flag. It was written in 1906. George M. Cohan wrote it.

George wrote the song after he met a Civil War veteran. When the two met, the man was holding a flag. Mr. Cohan saw that the flag looked very old. The man told him, "She's a grand old rag." George loved that line!

Mr. Cohan named the song "You're a Grand Old Rag." Many people didn't like the flag being called a rag. So George changed the title to "You're a Grand Old Flag."

1. According to the passage, in what year was "You're a Grand Old Flag" written?

   _____

2. According to the passage, why did George Cohan change the name of his song?

   _____

3. This is an **inference** question. The passage doesn't say, but why do you think people didn't like the flag being called a rag?

   a. people thought it didn't make any sense

   b. people thought the word rag didn't show respect for the flag

   c. people thought the word rag wouldn't rhyme well

   d. people thought the song's name should be shorter

4. This is another **inference** question. How did people feel about the song once George changed the name of it?

   a. they loved it

   b. they didn't like it

   c. the didn't care about it

   d. they were angry about the change

5. In this passage, <u>famous</u> means:

   _____

6. Put an X next to each statement that is a small *detail* from the passage about "You're a Grand Old Flag."

   1. _____ George M. Cohan wrote "You're a Grand Old Flag."

   2. _____ The veteran George met fought in the Civil War.

   3. _____ The song was written in 1906.

   4. _____ There are many songs about the US flag.

   5. _____ "You're a Grand Old Flag" is a very famous song.

Part E - Bonus - Pronouns

Read the passage about Chandler and Lee Ann. The pronouns **they**, **them**, and **their** refer to Chandler and Lee Ann. If you count the number of times Chandler and Lee Ann are referred to by their names, by **they**, by **them**, and by **their**, that will tell you how many total times this short passage mentions Chandler and Lee Ann.

Chandler and Lee Ann are twins. **They** are the same age, of course. Also, **they** are like best friends. **Their** parents, however, have always encouraged **them** to lead **their** own lives.

Chandler and Lee Ann don't try to dress alike. **They** have completely different hobbies. **They** enjoy playing different sports. **Their** teachers are surprised that **they** are good at different subjects. Although **they** are different in many ways, one thing **they** have in common is that a lot of people like **them.**

Chandler and Lee Ann: **2 +** they: **7 +** their: **3 +** them: **2 = 14** times this passage mentions Chandler and Lee Ann.

BONUS REVIEW

When you answer an **inference** question, you have to use information you read and information you probably already know.

The passage above is **mostly about** Chandler and Lee Ann. One **detail** about them is that they are twins.

Fiction comes from the imagination of the writer. A story about creatures from the planet Mars is **fiction** because there aren't any creatures on Mars.

Lesson 24

Part A - Vocabulary

Directions: After you read each model, choose the word from the list that could *best* replace the underlined word in the model sentence.

1. **Model:** I love making my baby sister <u>giggle</u>. I tell her jokes all the time.

   a. cry

   b. sing

   c. dance

   d. laugh

2. **Model:** The loud music made my head <u>ache</u>. It felt awful.

   a. swim

   b. itch

   c. hurt

   d. full

Part B - Parts of a Story

It is good to be able to remember the order of events in a story. The boxes below show the three parts of a story: the first thing that happened is in box 1, the second thing that happened is in box 2, and the third thing that happened is in box 3. First, look at the boxes, and then read the story.

Regine and her friend, Thomas, decided to swim out to a raft in the lake.	When they were about half way, Thomas started to get tired.	Regine decided to go back to shore and she helped Thomas until he could stand up in the water.
1	2	3

Part C- Parts of a Story

Directions: Read the passage, and then answer the questions.

It started to rain. Ginger was a smart enough dog to get out of the rain. She ran to the door of the house and began to bark very loudly. Her owner heard the barking and saw the rain. She put Ginger in the garage.

1	2	3

1. Which of these belongs in Box 2?

    a.   dog barks

    b.   starts to rain

    c.   dog goes in the garage

2. Which of these belongs in Box 1?

    a.   dog barks

    b.   starts to rain

    c.   dog goes in the garage

3. Which of these belongs in Box 3?

    a.   dog barks

    b.   starts to rain

    c.   dog goes in the garage

Part D - Memory Techniques

Write the missing names of the provinces next to the correct arrows on the map below. Select your answers from these names: British Columbia, Saskatchewan, Ontario, Nova Scotia, and Newfoundland & Labrador.

NOTE: Remember the chant from Lesson 23.

B - A - S

M - O - Q

3 N's and a P.E.I.

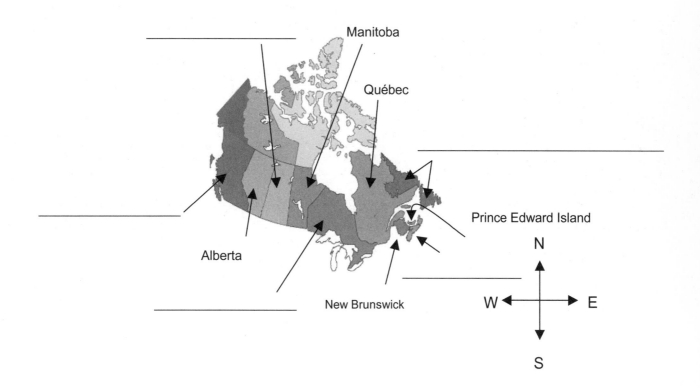

Part E- Review

Directions: Read the passage, and then answer the questions.

Last year, our class learned all about how to take care of plants. We planted sunflowers from seeds. We learned that plants and flowers need three things to grow: sun, water, and soil.

First, we planted the sunflower seeds in the soil. We had to make sure that there was a gap between each seed so that they weren't too crowded. Then, we had to water the seeds. We had to put all the seeds on the windowsill so that they would get plenty of light.

Our teacher let us check our plants every day. Because they were right in the sun, we had to water them every day. After a few weeks, we could see little plants start to grow above the soil. Some of our plants died, but most of them lived. By the end of the school year, our sunflowers were very tall and had blossomed. They took over the whole window and windowsill.

1. According to the passage, are sunflower plants big or small?

_____

2. What three things do plants need to live?

_____

3. This is an **inference** question. The passage doesn't say, but what do you think the students might have done with the sunflower plants at the end of the year?

    a. thrown them away

    b. taken them home to enjoy at their houses

    c. stopped watering them so that they died

    d. cut them up

4. This is another **inference** question. How would you feel if the sunflower you planted died?

    a. content

    b. proud

    c. lazy

    d. sad

5. In this passage, gap means:

_____

6. Put an X next to each statement that is a small *detail* from the passage about planting sunflowers.

1. _____ Sunflower seeds need to be planted with gaps between them.
2. _____ School is over at the end of June.
3. _____ Sunflowers grow very big and tall.
4. _____ Seeds, water, soil, and sunlight are all you need to grow sunflowers.
5. _____ Sunflowers need large spaces to grow.

Part F - Bonus - Pronouns

Read the passage about Samuel. The pronouns **he**, **him**, and **his** refer to Samuel. If you count the number of times Samuel is referred to by his name, by **he**, by **him**, and by **his**, that will tell you how many total times this short passage mentions Samuel.

Samuel is a turtle. **He** lives in the bedroom of **his** owner, Sherry. **Samuel** likes the way Sherry treats **him**. She feeds **him** good food regularly. She is very gentle with **him** when she picks **him** up. **He** likes the fact that Sherry doesn't let her friends pick **him** up, as well.

Samuel likes **his** home, too. **His** home is an aquarium. It's full of the things that turtles like **Samuel** enjoy, such as water and shade. Maybe most dogs have a good life, but **Samuel** is a happy turtle, thanks to **his** owner.

Samuel: **5 +** he: **2 +** him: **5 +** his: **4 = 16** times this passage mentions Samuel.

BONUS REVIEW

You have to gather evidence, like a detective, when you answer **inference** questions. Some of that evidence is in the reading passage and some is information you probably already know.

The passage above is **mostly about** Samuel. One **detail** about him is that he lives in an aquarium.

Fiction comes from the imagination of the writer. It might have true facts in it, but the story is make-believe.

Lesson 26

Part A - Vocabulary

Directions: Write the words from below that fit the definitions.

giggle

ache

miserable

ancient

bargain

1. Mark was _____ about his grade on the science test. He thought that he had studied enough, but he was wrong.

2. The clowns at the circus are so funny. I always _____ when I see them.

3. I ate popcorn, peanuts, hot dogs, and cotton candy at the baseball game. I think all that food made my stomach _____.

4. My science teacher told me that alligators are _____. They've been around for over 200 million years.

5. A great way to get a _____ is to wait to go shopping until the end of every season.

Part B - Reading Subject Matter Books

Sometimes, we read for **enjoyment**. We enjoy reading a good story. Many times, we **read to learn**. For example, when we read a science book, we are reading to learn more about science.

When we read **fiction**, we start at the beginning and read every page after that. When we **read to learn**, however, we don't necessarily have to start at the beginning and read every page. You are going to learn some good methods for **reading to learn**.

Part C- Reading Subject Matter Books

Directions: Read the information below from a science book, and then follow your teacher's instructions.

Name of Book: General Science Today

Table of Contents:

Unit 1...............Classification of Animals

Unit 2...............The Human Body

Unit 3...............Light and Optics

Unit 4...............Sound

Unit 5...............Ecology

Unit 6...............Astronomy

1. The title of this book tells us what the whole book is about. What is this book about?

2. What do you already know about science?

3. Why might this book be called General Science Today?

4. What is Unit 2 about?

5. What kinds of things do you think Unit 2 might tell us about?

Part D- Parts of a Story

Directions: Read the passage, and then answer the questions.

It was finally time for our vacation. First we took all of our luggage and got on the bus. Then, we got on a train. The train took us to the airport where we got on a plane to Florida. We were so excited to visit Disney World!

1	2	3

1. Which of these belongs in Box 3?

    a. got on a plane

    b. got on a bus

    c. got on a train

2. Which of these belongs in Box 2?

    a. got on a bus

    b. got on a plane

    c. got on a train

3. Which of these belongs in Box 1?

    a. got on a train

    b. got on a bus

    c. got on a plane

Part E- Review

Directions: Read the passage, and then answer the questions.

People started going to space in the 1960s. The first American in space was Alan Shepard, Jr. He flew into space on May 5, 1961. He flew a spacecraft named *Freedom 7*. He was in space for 15 minutes.

John Glenn, Jr. was the first American to <u>orbit</u> the earth. On February 20, 1962, he orbited the earth three times. He flew on the *Friendship 7*.

People always wanted to go to the moon. On July 20, 1969, the first person from Earth landed on the moon. His name was Neil Armstrong. He was an American. The name of his spacecraft was *Apollo 11*. It's probably the most famous spacecraft ever.

1. According to the passage, who was the first American in space?

_____

2. Who flew on *Freedom 7*?

_____

3. This is an **inference** question. The passage doesn't say, but why do you think people always wanted to go to the moon?

    a.   staying on Earth was boring

    b.   the moon is close to the earth

    c.   it was a great accomplishment

    d.   it was easy

4. This is another **inference** question. Why is *Apollo 11* probably the most famous spacecraft ever?

    a.   it was the first spacecraft to land on the moon

    b.   it came after *Freedom 7*

    c.   John Glenn, Jr. flew it

    d.   it was made in America

5. In this passage, <u>orbit</u> means:

_____

6. Put an X next to each statement that is a small *detail* from the passage about space flight.

    1. _____ Alan Shepard, Jr. was the first American in space.

    2. _____ Very few people have flown in space.

    3. _____ John Glenn, Jr. was the first American to orbit the earth.

    4. _____ Alan Shepard. Jr. was only in space for 15 minutes.

    5. _____ John Glenn, Jr. orbited the earth three times.

Part F - Bonus - Pronouns

Read the passage about "Markus and I." The pronouns **we**, **us**, and **our** refer to "Markus and I". We don't know the name of the person telling the story. If you count the number of times "Markus and I" are referred to just by **we**, by **us**, and by **our**, that will tell you how many total times this short passage mentions "Markus and I," not counting the name Markus and the pronoun I.

Markus and I play on the same soccer team. **We** have been on the same team for three years. **Our** coach is the same coach **we** had when **we** started. She is nice to **us**, and she has taught **us** a lot in three years. When **we** aren't playing soccer, **we** are talking about it. Obviously, **our** favorite pastime is soccer.

we: **5+** us: **2 +** our: **2 = 9** times this passage mentions Markus and the person telling the story.

BONUS REVIEW

The passage above is **mostly about** Markus and the person telling the story. One **detail** about them is that they have had the same coach for three years.

Fiction comes from the imagination of the writer.

Lesson 27

Part A - Vocabulary

Directions: After you read each model, choose the word from the list that could *best* replace the underlined word in the model sentence.

1. **Model:** I try not to argue with people. I think any problem can be talked through.

   a. fight

   b. sing

   c. laugh

   d. cry

2. **Model:** To make a milk shake, you have to blend ice cream and milk. Ice cream and milk taste great together!

   a. freeze

   b. hold

   c. turn

   d. mix

Part B- Reading Subject Matter Books

Directions: Read the information below from a science book, and then follow your teacher's instructions.

Name of Book: General Science Today

Table of Contents:

Unit 1...............Classification of Animals

Unit 2...............The Human Body

Chapter 1: The Muscle System

Chapter 2: The Skeletal System

Chapter 3: The Nervous System

Chapter 4: Vision

Chapter 5: Hearing

Unit 3...............Light and Optics

Unit 4...............Sound

Unit 5...............Ecology

Unit 6...............Astronomy

1. What does the title of this book tell us?

2. What is Unit 2 about?

3. The word "skeletal" is related to the word "skeleton." What is Unit 2, Chapter 2 probably about?

4. What human organs would you be reading about in Unit 2, Chapter 4?

5. What human organs would you be reading about in Unit 2, Chapter 5?

6. What do you already know about muscles?

Part C - Memory Techniques

Write the missing names of the provinces next to the correct arrows on the map below. Select your answers from these names: Manitoba, Saskatchewan, Ontario, New Brunswick, Alberta, Nova Scotia, and Prince Edward Island.

NOTE: Remember the chant from Lesson 23.

B - A - S

M - O - Q

3 N's and a P.E.I.

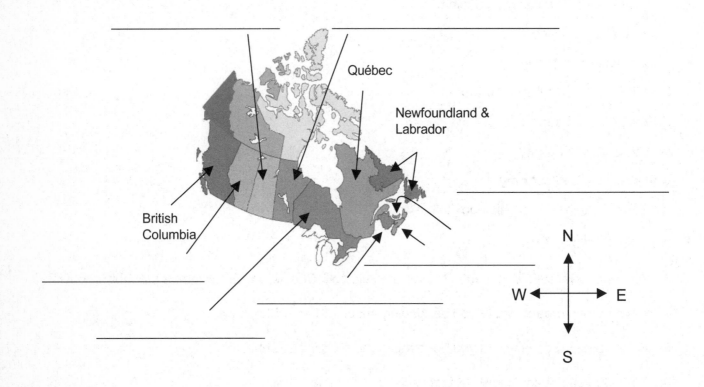

Part D- Review

Directions: Read the passage, and then answer the questions.

For Navajo Native Americans, sand painting is important. It is both an <u>ancient</u> art and part of their ceremonies. In sand painting, the artist or healer makes a picture. The picture is made of colored sand or crushed stone. In a ceremony, this picture is made on the ground. To make a piece of art to be sold, the painting is made on wood.

Navajos learned sand painting from the Pueblo Native Americans. The Pueblos learned it from their prehistoric ancestors. Sand paintings can be very large or very small. Most sand paintings are between six and eight feet. The colors used most in sand paintings are red, white, blue, yellow, and black.

Sand paintings are used in ceremonies that restore the balance between good and evil. They are also used in the Blessing Way Ceremony. This ceremony is performed when a celebration is held. Outsiders rarely see these sand paintings. They are made in one day and then destroyed at night. The Navajos don't need them anymore after harmony has been restored or a blessing has been given.

1. According to the passage, who did the Navajo learn sand painting from?

_____

2. What colors are used most in sand painting?

_____

3. This is an **inference** question. The passage doesn't say, but why do you think balance might need to be restored in a Navajo ceremony?

    a.   it is raining

    b.   it is night

    c.   someone is sick

    d.   the seasons change

4. This is another **inference** question. Why do outsiders rarely get to see a Navajo ceremony with a sand painting?

    a.   the Navajos are embarrassed

    b.   it is a sacred event only for Navajos

    c.   there is not enough room for everyone

    d.   they can't afford to invite everyone

5. In this passage, <u>ancient</u> means:

    _____

6. Put an X next to each statement that is a small *detail* from the passage about Navajo sand paintings.

    1. _____ Many Navajos live in Arizona.
    2. _____ Ceremonial sand paintings are destroyed at night.
    3. _____ Sand paintings are made from colored sand or crushed rock.
    4. _____ Most sand paintings are between six and eight feet.
    5. _____ Outsiders rarely see sand paintings.

Part F - Bonus - Pronouns

Read the passage about the alligator. The pronouns **it** and **its** refer to the alligator. If you count the number of times the alligator is referred to by its name, by **it**, and by **its**, that will tell you how many total times this short passage mentions the alligator.

> I saw **the alligator** the moment our boat turned into a shady area. **It** was gigantic. All of us stayed away from **it** by standing away from the edges of the boat. Our guide threw some marshmallows into the water. **The alligator** swam toward them and instantly gulped them down into **its** huge mouth. We could see **its** huge teeth when it opened **its** mouth. After a while, **the alligator** swam to the shore and disappeared.

the alligator: **3** it: **2 +** its: **3 = 8** times this passage mentions the alligator.

BONUS REVIEW

The passage above is **mostly about** the alligator. One **detail** about it is that it swam to the shore.

You use the knowledge you already have and information from a passage to answer an **inference** question.

Lesson 28

Part A - Vocabulary

Directions: Write the words from below that fit the definitions.

ached

giggling

argue

blend

brief

1. When my mom makes cookies, she uses a hand mixer to
_____ everything together.

2. My arms _____ for a week after tennis practice.

3. I hate when my friends _____. I like it much better when everyone gets along.

4. When my daddy tickles me, I can't stop _____.

5. We had a _____ spelling test on Friday. It was only five words long.

Part B- Reading Subject Matter Books

Directions: Read the information below from a science book, and then follow your teacher's instructions.

Name of Book: General Science Today

Table of Contents:

1. What is Unit 2, Chapter 1 probably about?

2. What do you know about muscles?

3. Muscles are attached to different parts of our bodies. What part of our bodies do you think skeletal muscles are attached to? **Hint**: Skeletal means anything having to do with your bones.

4. Where do you think you find Cardiac Muscles? **Hint**: Cardiac means anything having to do with your heart.

5. What are some ways you can think of to take care of your muscles?

Part C- Parts of a Story

Directions: Read the passage, and then answer the questions.

My sister had a baby the other day. That means that I am now an uncle. After the baby was born we bought my sister some flowers and took them to the hospital. My sister was happy to see us and I got to hold my new nephew.

1	2	3

1. Which of these belongs in Box 2?

    a. baby was born

    b. bought some flowers

    c. went to the hospital

2. Which of these belongs in Box 3?

    a. went to the hospital

    b. baby was born

    c. bought some flowers

3. Which of these belongs in Box 1?

    a. bought some flowers

    b. went to the hospital

    c. baby was born

Part D- Review

Directions: Read the passage, and then answer the questions.

You probably eat french fries all the time. But, how much do you really know about potatoes? The Incas in Peru first started growing potatoes around 200 B.C. That is a long time ago! A Spanish explorer named Castellanos saw the Incas growing and eating potatoes when he was in Peru. He brought them back to Europe.

At first, only the royalty in Europe were willing to try the potato. Many people thought that the potato was evil and caused disease. Because many kings liked the potato so much, soon they forced all the people to start growing and eating potatoes. Potatoes became very popular in Europe. Europeans sent <u>crates</u> of potatoes to the new colony in Jamestown in 1691. People in New England began to grow their own potatoes in 1719.

Today, the potato is the most popular vegetable in America. Potatoes are very nutritious. They have lots of fiber, vitamin C, and potassium. Every American eats about 126 pounds of potatoes each year. Idaho grows the most potatoes of any state in the U.S. The most popular ways to eat potatoes in America are baked, followed by mashed and french fries.

1. According to the passage, what state in the U.S. grows the most potatoes?

_____

2. What vitamins and nutrients do potatoes have?

_____

3. This is an **inference** question. The passage doesn't say, but why do you think people in Europe first thought that potatoes were evil and caused disease?

    a.   they were brown

    b.   the royalty liked them

    c.   the Incas told them potatoes would make them sick

    d.   they were scared of something new

4. This is another **inference** question. Why do you think Castellanos brought potatoes from Peru back to Europe with him?

    a.   he thought they tasted good

    b.   he wanted to make everyone in Europe sick

    c.   he wanted something heavy to put in his ship

    d.   he wanted to steal from the Incas

5. In this passage, <u>crates</u> means:

_____

6. Put an X next to each statement that is a small *detail* from the passage about potatoes.

1. _____ At first, Europeans did not want to eat potatoes.
2. _____ Potatoes were first grown in Peru.
3. _____ Potatoes are the most popular vegetable in America.
4. _____ Potatoes were sent to Jamestown from Europe.
5. _____ In the 1840's there was a potato famine in Ireland.

Part E - Bonus - Pronouns

All the words below are **pronouns**:

I	me	my
you	they	your
it	their	its
she	them	her
he	him	his
we	us	our

Pronouns refer to people and things. When you count the number of times a passage talks about people or things, you are counting **pronouns**.

BONUS REVIEW

Fiction comes from the imagination of the person who writes it.

You can't find the exact answer to an **inference** question in a passage.

Lesson 29

Part A- Reading Subject Matter Books-Word Pronunciation

Directions: Below are some vocabulary words from a book chapter about the muscle system. Your teacher will read each word for you and then will ask you to pronounce it.

1. **contracting** (cun TRAKT ing)

2. **voluntary** (VOL un tear ee)

3. **involuntary** (in VOL un tear ee)

4. **elastic** (UH las tik)

5. **cardiac** (CAR dee ak)

6. **skeletal** (SKELL ut tul)

7. **digest** (die JEST)

8. **vessels** (VES uls)

9. **deltoids** (DELL toydz)

10. **rectus abdominus** (RECK tus ab DOM un us)

11. **biceps** (BYE seps)

12. **tendons** (TEN dunz)

13. **aerobic** (air OH bick)

Part B- Memory Techniques

Directions: Write the name of each Great Lake.

Hint: The name of the largest lake can mean "big" or "large" or "best."

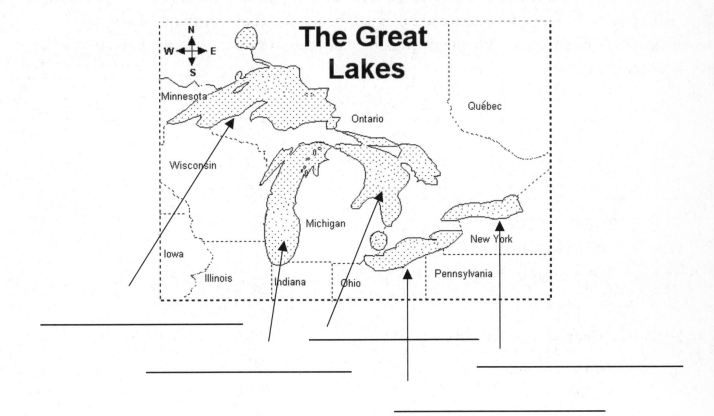

_____

_____

_____

_____

Part C- Parts of a Story

Directions: Read the passage, and then answer the questions.

Every Thursday afternoon, my grandmother takes my sisters and me to the library. We have a routine. My sisters and I pick out books and check them out. Then, we get to go for ice cream. When my grandmother brings us home, she stays at our house for dinner.

1	2	3

1. Which of these belongs in Box 1?

    a. go home for dinner

    b. pick out books

    c. get ice cream

2. Which of these belongs in Box 3?

    a. pick out books

    b. get ice cream

    c. go home for dinner

3. Which of these belongs in Box 2?

    a. get ice cream

    b. go home for dinner

    c. pick out books

Part D- Review

Directions: Read the passage, and then answer the questions.

The duck-billed platypus is a fascinating animal. The platypus is a mammal, but it has characteristics of both mammals and reptiles. It is almost like a <u>blend</u> of a reptile and a mammal. While the platypus lays eggs like a reptile, it has hair and can breathe through lungs like a mammal.

A platypus is about the size of a small cat. The platypus is a pretty funny looking animal. The body of a platypus looks like a groundhog, but it has a tail like a beaver and a bill like a duck! Their feet are webbed like a duck's feet. The male platypus is the only furry mammal that has poisonous venom. The venom is found in the claws of the male platypus.

Platypuses live in Australia. They live in burrows near rivers and streams. They dive into the water to find their food. Platypuses like to eat worms, snails, and shrimp. They can even make noise. The noise they make sounds like a puppy growling. These strange animals live to be between ten and fifteen years old.

1. According to the passage, how old do platypuses usually grow to be?

_____

2. What do platypuses eat?

_____

3. This is an **inference** question. The passage doesn't say, but why do you think the author thinks that platypuses are funny looking?

    a. they have parts that look like many different kinds of animals

    b. other animals don't like them

    c. they always hide so you can't see what they look like

    d. they make funny faces

4. This is another **inference** question. What do you think the male platypus uses his venom for?

    a. to dig in the mud

    b. to scratch his fur

    c. to protect himself from enemies

    d. to swim

5. In this passage, <u>blend</u> means:

_____

6. Put an X next to each statement that is a small *detail* from the passage about the platypus.

    1. _____ Platypuses are funny looking animals.

    2. _____ A platypus is about the size of a cat.

    3. _____ Platypuses are only found in Australia.

    4. _____ Platypuses live next to rivers and streams.

    5. _____ The platypus has four legs.

Part E - Bonus - Pronouns

All the words below are **pronouns**:

I	me	my
you	their	your
it	they	its
she	them	her
he	him	his
we	us	our

Pronouns refer to people and things.

BONUS REVIEW

Fiction comes from the imagination of the person who writes it. Sometimes, **fiction** is written so realistically that it seems like fact. Even then, though, the story comes from the writer's imagination.

You can't find the exact answer to an **inference** question in a passage. You have to use information from the passage as well as some knowledge you already have.

Lesson 31

Part A - Vocabulary

Directions: After you read each model, choose the word from the list that could *best* replace the underlined word in the model sentence.

1. **Model:** We had to put my dog in a plastic <u>crate</u> when we took him on the plane. We had to lock it to make sure he didn't get out.

    a. box

    b. chair

    c. car

    d. room

2. **Model:** I <u>donned</u> my best coat to go out for dinner for my birthday. I was happy it was cold enough to wear a coat.

    a. took off

    b. threw out

    c. put on

    d. washed

Part B- Memory Techniques

Directions: Write the name of each Great Lake.

_____

_____

_____ _____

_____

Part C- Parts of a Story

Directions: Read the passage, and then answer the questions.

When I had the flu, I was so sick that I had to stay home for a whole week. During that time, I got used to the neighborhood schedule. I knew when everyone left for work or school. At about 7 a.m. the paper boy would deliver the paper. At about noon, the mail carrier delivered the mail. Finally, at 2:30 p.m. the school bus dropped off all my friends from school.

1	2	3

1. Which of these belongs in Box 1?

    a.   school bus drops off students

    b.   paper delivered

    c.   mail is delivered

2. Which of these belongs in Box 3?

    a.   paper is delivered

    b.   mail is delivered

    c.   school bus drops off students

3. Which of these belongs in Box 2?

    a.   mail is delivered

    b.   paper is delivered

    c.   school bus drops off students

Part D- Review

Directions: Read the passage, and then answer the questions.

Do you have a dream of becoming an Olympic athlete? Do you know anything about the history of the Olympics? The first Olympic games were held in 776 B.C.

At the first Olympics there was only one event - the 210 yard race. The first Olympics were held in Olympia, Greece. The Olympics were then held every four years until they were stopped. The Roman emperor Theodosius I stopped them in 393.

Many years later the Olympics were started again. The first modern Olympics were held in 1896 in Athens, Greece. There were 300 athletes from 13 countries. They competed in 9 events. Since then the Olympics has started many new traditions. Today, in the opening ceremonies, each country's athletes march under their own banner.

In 2004 the summer Olympics were held in Athens once again. This time there were athletes from 202 countries competing in 35 events.

1. According to the passage, when were the first Olympics held?

    _____

2. Where were the first **modern** Olympics held?

    _____

3. Why do you think the Olympics are held every four years?

    a.   no one wants to watch it each year

    b.   it is tradition

    c.   it takes that long to travel to the games

    d.   four is an even number

4. When do you think the opening ceremonies of the Olympics take place?

    a.   a month before the games start

    b.   on the last day

    c.   when someone wins a medal

    d.   on the first day

5. In this passage, <u>banner</u> means:

_____

6. Put an X next to each statement that is a small *detail* from the passage about the Olympics.
    1. _____ The first Olympics were held in 776 B.C.
    2. _____ Theodosius I stopped the Olympics in 393 A.D.
    3. _____ The 2004 Olympics were held in Athens.
    4. _____ The 1896 Olympics were held in Athens.
    5. _____ The International Olympic Committee runs the Olympics.

Part E - Bonus

You know that **fiction** comes from the imagination of a writer. When writing is true or factual, it is called **nonfiction**. A book about playing soccer is **nonfiction**. A recipe book is **nonfiction**. A true story about a person's life is **nonfiction**.

BONUS REVIEW

Remember that all the words below are **pronouns**:

I	me	my
you	him	your
it	us	its
she	them	her
he	they	his
we	their	our

Pronouns refer to people and things.

A **detail** is a small part of something.

Lesson 32

Part A - Vocabulary

Directions: Write the words from below that fit the definitions.

crate

donned

argue

blend

gap

1. My grandma sent us fruit and it came in a wooden
   _____.

2. My dentist said I need braces because of the _____
   between my two front teeth.

3. My sister and I never _____. She's my best friend.

4. When my dad asked me to help him work in the garden, I
   _____ a pair of old jeans.

5. I like all kinds of music, so I like radio stations that play a
   _____ of everything.

Part B - Reading Subject Matter Books

Directions: Below is all of Chapter 1 from Unit 2 of the book, *General Science Today*. You are not going to read the whole chapter in today's lesson.

Instead, you are just going to read _the first paragraph_ after each heading. After you read the first paragraph after a heading, answer the questions for that paragraph.

The first paragraph and the questions for that paragraph are in boxes.

Introduction

Your muscles are very important. Muscles do the same thing as a car engine. They turn energy into motion. Muscles move and make you capable of moving by **contracting** (cun TRAKT ing) and becoming shorter. Muscles pull, but they cannot push. Without your muscles you wouldn't be able to do most things. You wouldn't be able to play an instrument, throw a baseball, walk, talk or even smile. Your heart also wouldn't be able to pump blood through your body. People have over 650 muscles in our bodies. All of them have very important jobs to do.

1. When a muscle pulls and becomes shorter, that is called:

   _____

2. Which job do muscles **not** do?

   a.   make it possible for you to walk

   b.   pump blood through your body

   c.   do math problems

   d.   make it possible for you to play a sport

3. How many muscles do we have in our bodies?

   _____

Some muscles in our bodies work on their own, without us ever thinking about it. These muscles are called **involuntary** (in VOL un ter ee) muscles. Some muscles in our bodies we can control. These muscles are called **voluntary** (VOL un ter ee) muscles.

Muscles make up about half of your body weight. That means if you weigh 70 pounds, about 35 pounds of you is muscle. All muscles are made of the same thing. They are made of hundreds and thousands of small **elastic** (UH las tik) fibers.

People have three kinds of muscles: **cardiac** (CAR dee ak) muscles, smooth muscles, and **skeletal** (SKELL it ull) muscles.

Cardiac Muscles

Cardiac muscles are found only in the heart. They create the power that pumps blood through your body. Cardiac muscles contract to pump blood out of the heart. Then, they relax to let blood back into the heart.

4. Which two things are true about your heart?

    a. it is a pump

    b. it is a skeletal muscle

    c. it is made of muscles

Cardiac muscles are involuntary muscles. That means that your brain and nervous system tell the cardiac muscles what to do. They do it without you ever thinking about it. Think about how many times each day your cardiac muscles pump blood through your body without you ever thinking about it!

Smooth Muscles

You know that cardiac muscles are involuntary muscles. Smooth muscles are also involuntary muscles. They help our bodies in many different ways.

5. Are smooth muscles voluntary or involuntary?

_____

Smooth muscles surround or are part of your organs. Smooth muscles are in your stomach, helping you to **digest** (die JEST) food. They are in your bladder, helping you control when you urinate. They are in your blood **vessels** helping to deliver blood throughout your body. They are also in your airways, helping you breathe. Smooth muscles are found in many parts of your body helping your body do the things that keep you healthy every day.

Skeletal Muscles

Skeletal muscles are the kind of muscles most of us know about. They are the muscles that help us kick a soccer ball. Skeletal muscles are voluntary muscles. That means that they are muscles that we control. Your leg won't kick a soccer ball unless you want it to!

6. A *voluntary* muscle is a muscle you can:

_____

7. When we say someone is strong, we are probably talking about what type of muscle?

    a.   smooth

    b.   cardiac

    c.   skeletal

Working with your bones, skeletal muscles give you power and strength. Usually skeletal muscles are attached to one end of a bone. They stretch across a joint and attach to the end of another bone.

Like all muscles, skeletal muscles work by contracting. When you bend your leg to kick a soccer ball, the skeletal muscles in the back of your thigh contract and they pull your leg bones up and back.

Some skeletal muscles are big, like the ones in your back that help to keep you standing straight and tall. Some skeletal muscles are smaller, like the ones in your neck that help you turn your head from side to side.

There are many skeletal muscles. There are almost too many to name. Some of the more important skeletal muscles you've probably heard of already.

Your shoulder muscles are called **deltoids** (DELL toydz). These muscles help you move your shoulders around and around.

Under your ribs are your **rectus abdominus** (RECK tuss ab DOM in uss) muscles. You've probably heard them called "abs." These muscles help you do sit-ups.

When you make a muscle with your arm, the muscle that you see push up under the skin of your upper arm is called your **biceps** (BYE seeps).

Tendons

Tendons (TEN dunz) help to hold skeletal muscles to bones. Tendons are tough cords, like ropes. They work like connector pieces between bones and muscles.

8. What do tendons connect?

_____

9. Tendons are like:

    a.   rope

    b.   muscles

    c.   bones

There are parts of your body that are small and are made up of very small bones, like your hands, fingers, feet and toes. Muscles wouldn't fit in these places. Specially shaped tendons extend all the way to the tips of your fingers and toes and connect the bones there to muscles higher up in your arms and legs. You really have no muscles in your fingers. You can move them because of tendons working together with muscles in your arms.

Taking Care of Your Muscles

Your muscles do very important things. They keep your heart beating and they let you move your body. Because they are so important, it's important to take care of them.

10. What two important things do your muscles do?

_____

To keep your cardiac and skeletal muscles healthy and strong, you should try **aerobic** (air OH bick) exercise. Aerobic exercise is exercise that brings in oxygen to your skeletal muscles. Exercises like swimming, jogging, and roller blading are aerobic exercises. When you bring in more oxygen, your cardiac muscles become stronger and more powerful.

If you want to make your skeletal muscles bigger and stronger, try things like push-ups, crunches, pull-ups, and bike riding.

Part C - Bonus

Remember, when writing is true or factual, it is called **nonfiction**. A book about getting along better with people is **nonfiction**. The articles in an encyclopedia are **nonfiction**. A story you write about something that actually happened to you is **nonfiction**.

BONUS REVIEW

The opposite of **nonfiction** is **fiction**.

Some **pronouns** are: she, he, him, her, his, and hers.

You can't find the exact answer to an **inference** question in a passage.

Lesson 33

Part A - Counting Pronouns

Directions: Read the story below. Count the number of times the pronouns *she*, *her*, and *hers* are used to refer to Alexa.

Alexa likes to work for free in her community. Some weekends, she helps clean up garbage along the road. At other times, she visits people in a nursing home and talks to the older people there. Those people look forward to her coming for a visit. Some of them don't get many visitors. People tell Alexa that she is doing a great job. She always says that the pleasure is hers.

Total number of times that she, her, and hers refer to Alexa: _____
Note: this passage is **mostly about** Alexa and some things she does.

Part B - Parts of a Story

Directions: Read the story below and then follow the directions after the story.

Jackie is great with words. She is very good at spelling. Last year she entered our school's spelling bee. She came in second. The girl who beat her was three years older than she was. Jackie is trying again this year. She practices spelling new words every day. She gets to school early in the morning and practices in the cafeteria. Then, during recess, she practices on the playground. After school she practices in the library. She's sure to win this year.

Box 1 shows one thing that happened in this story. Box 3 shows something else from the story.

Box 2 is empty. Something that happened *between* Box 1 and Box 3 goes in Box 2. One thing that happened between Jackie practicing spelling in the cafeteria and Jackie practicing spelling in the library is "practices on playground."

practices in cafeteria		practices in library
1	2	3

Part C- Parts of a Story

Directions: Read the passage, and then answer the question.

NOTE: This story has more than three parts.

Aiden was in a hurry. He was late for a meeting with his video club. Every Saturday his club got together and made video tapes with a friend's video camera. They loaded their videos on to a computer and made movie from them.

Before he could leave, though, he had to finish his breakfast. Next, he had some Saturday morning chores he had to do. The chores included feeding the cat and making his bed. Finally, he was able to leave for the club meeting.

Aiden was late, but the meeting went on longer than usual, anyway. His friends were working on a funny movie about a neighbor's dog. The dog could jump through a hoop and catch a ball in mid-air. Sometimes, though, the dog would miss the ball. Then he would bark like crazy. It looked like the dog was angry because someone made a bad throw.

did chores		arrived late
1	2	3

1. Which of these belongs in Box 2? That is, which event happened *between* the thing in Box 1 and the thing in Box 3?

    a. dog got angry

    b. ate breakfast

    c. left for meeting

    d. worked on funny movie

Part D- Review

Directions: Read the passage, and then answer the questions.

Origami is folding paper to create figures. It is a kind of art. Many times the figures are animals, objects, people, or shapes. The paper is folded to make three dimensional pieces. That means that the pieces are not flat. The word origami comes from Japanese words that mean "to fold paper."

You can use almost any paper to create origami. The best paper to use is thin but strong. That is because it holds <u>creases</u> well. Usually origami paper is cut into six inch squares. The paper is printed on one side and white on the other side.

If you want to learn to do origami you have to learn the four most common "base" folds first. Those folds are: the kite base, the fish base, the bird base, and the frog base. If you know those four folds, you can have fun making all kinds of origami!

1. According to the passage, what language does the word "origami" come from?

    _____

2. What are two of the four most common base folds in origami?

    _____

3. Why do you think you need to know the four common base folds in order to do origami?

    a.   so that you can make harder folds

    b.   so that you can pass the test

    c.   so that you can pick the right paper

    d.   so that you can learn Japanese

4. Where do you think origami was invented?

    a.   Brazil

    b.   Germany

    c.   Japan

    d.   United States

5. In this passage, <u>creases</u> means:

_____

6. Put an X next to each statement that is a small *detail* from the passage about origami.

    1. _____ There are four common base folds in origami.

    2. _____ The word origami comes from the Japanese language.

    3. _____ Some origami artists use cardboard for their designs.

    4. _____ Most origami paper is cut into six inch squares.

    5. _____ You need thin, strong paper for origami.

Part E - Bonus

Remember, when writing is true or factual, it is called **nonfiction**. A history book is **nonfiction**. The articles in an encyclopedia are **nonfiction**. A science book is **nonfiction**. The passage about origami in Part D is **nonfiction**.

BONUS REVIEW

The opposite of **nonfiction** is **fiction**.

Some **pronouns** are: they, them, we, us, their, and our.

A **detail** is a small part of something.

Lesson 34

Part A - Counting Pronouns

Directions: Read the story below. Count the number of times the pronouns *they*, *them*, and *their* are used to refer to Luis and Samantha.

Luis and Samantha are best friends. They want a new hobby. They thought about gardening. But what would they do in the winter? They thought about painting but that can be messy. They asked their mothers to give them an opinion. Their moms suggested puzzles. They went to the store and saw there were a lot of puzzles. They both like big ships and there were at least 5 puzzles with pictures of ships. They love camping too. They found at least 10 puzzles with pictures of the outdoors. They decided that puzzles are the perfect new hobby for them.

Total number of times that they, them, and their refer to Luis and Samantha: _____
Note: this passage is **mostly about** Luis and Samantha and their search for a new hobby.

Part B - Vocabulary (Matching)

Directions: Find the definitions from the box that match the words below.

a.	a type of box
b.	hurts
c.	mix together
d.	very unhappy
e.	very old

Write the letter of the definition that matches each word.

1. miserable _____

2. crate _____

3. aches _____

4. blend _____

5. ancient _____

Part C- Reading Subject Matter Books

When you read a chapter from a book, you should read the questions at the end of the chapter *before* you read the chapter. That helps you focus on the most important parts of the chapter.

In the next lesson, you're going to read the questions at the end of the science chapter on muscles. You aren't going to read the passage in this lesson, and you aren't going to answer the questions. You're just going to read the questions and then try to remember as many of them as you can.

Part D- Reading Subject Matter Books (Continued)

Directions: Read the questions below from the end of the science chapter on muscles, and then close your workbook.

1. What do we call muscles that we can control ourselves?
2. What do we call muscles that we can **not** control ourselves?
3. Name the three types of muscles.
4. What kind of muscle is your heart?
5. What type of muscle surrounds the stomach and blood vessels?
6. The muscles that move your arms and legs are what type of muscle?
7. Which muscle group is **not** below your ribs?
8. What attaches muscles to bones?
9. Your muscles do what two important things?
10. Aerobic exercise helps strengthen which two types of muscles?

Part E - Bonus

Remember, when writing is true or factual, it is called **nonfiction**. The chapter about muscles is **nonfiction**. A story about someone's life is **nonfiction**.

BONUS REVIEW

The opposite of **nonfiction** is **fiction**.

Some **pronouns** are: her, their, our, his, its, and your.

Lesson 36

Part A - Parts of a Story

Directions: Read the story below and then follow the directions after the story.

Jack has a baby sister. On weekends, their parents let Jack help with the baby. Jack feeds the baby oatmeal for breakfast. Then they go to the park. The baby loves the swings. When they get home, Jack fixes her a snack. It's usually mashed bananas. Before dinner, Jack puts on a puppet show for her. Jack's favorite thing comes just before bed. Before the baby goes to sleep, Jack reads her Winnie the Pooh.

Box 1 shows one thing that happened in this story. Box 3 shows something else from the story.

Box 2 is empty. Something that happened *between* Box 1 and Box 3 goes in Box 2. One thing that happened between feeding the baby oatmeal and fixing a snack is: "going to park."

feeding baby oatmeal		fixing baby a snack
1	2	3

Part B- Parts of a Story

Directions: Read the passage, and then answer the question.

NOTE: This story has more than three parts.

With four kids in a family, plus a dog, things can get really busy. Sometimes at the end of a weekend we wonder where all the time went. For instance, last weekend we had a million things to do.

On Saturday morning we had to run some errands. Then we had to take the dog to the park. At 2:00 my brother Tim had a soccer game. At 4:30 my sister Ava had a birthday party to go to. After that, we went to the video store to get a movie. Then we picked up a pizza for dinner

On Sunday we had to wake up early for a family party about an hour away. Later, my brother Jackson had a baseball practice. By the time we got home, we were almost too tired to eat dinner.

take the dog to the park		birthday party
1	2	3

1. Which of these belongs in Box 2? That is, which event happened *between* the thing in Box 1 and the thing in Box 3?

    a. soccer game

    b. family party

    c. baseball practice

    d. picked up pizza

Part C - Reading Subject Matter Books

Directions: You are going to read the chapter below on muscles. First, however, look at the questions at the end of the chapter. Then read the chapter.

In another lesson, you will actually answer the questions at the end of the chapter.

Introduction

Your muscles are very important. Muscles do the same thing as a car engine. They turn energy into motion. Muscles move and make you capable of moving by **contracting** (cun TRAKT ing) and becoming shorter. Muscles pull, but they cannot push. Without your muscles you wouldn't be able to do most things. You wouldn't be able to play an instrument, throw a baseball, walk, talk or even smile. Your heart also wouldn't be able to pump blood through your body. People have over 650 muscles in our bodies. All of them have very important jobs to do.

Some muscles in our bodies work on their own, without us ever thinking about it. These muscles are called **involuntary** (in VOL un ter ee) muscles. Some muscles in our bodies we can control. These muscles are called **voluntary** (VOL un ter ee) muscles.

Muscles make up about half of your body weight. That means if you weigh 70 pounds, about 35 pounds of you is muscle. All muscles are made of the same thing. They are made of hundreds and thousands of small **elastic** (UH las tik) fibers.

People have three kinds of muscles: **cardiac** (CAR dee ak) muscles, smooth muscles, and **skeletal** (SKELL it ull) muscles.

Cardiac Muscles

Cardiac muscles are found only in the heart. They create the power that pumps blood through your body. Cardiac muscles contract to pump blood out of the heart. Then, they relax to let blood back into the heart.

Cardiac muscles are involuntary muscles. That means that your brain and nervous system tell the cardiac muscles what to do. They do it without you ever thinking about it. Think about how many times each day your cardiac muscles pump blood through your body without you ever thinking about it!

Smooth Muscles

You know that cardiac muscles are involuntary muscles. Smooth muscles are also involuntary muscles. They help our bodies in many different ways.

Smooth muscles surround or are part of your organs. Smooth muscles are in your stomach, helping you to **digest** (die JEST) food. They are in your bladder, helping you control when you urinate. They are in your blood **vessels** helping to deliver blood throughout your body. They are also in your airways, helping you breathe. Smooth muscles are found in many parts of your body helping your body do the things that keep you healthy every day.

Skeletal Muscles

Skeletal muscles are the kind of muscles most of us know about. They are the muscles that help us kick a soccer ball. Skeletal muscles are voluntary muscles. That means that they are muscles that we control. Your leg won't kick a soccer ball unless you want it to!

Working with your bones, skeletal muscles give you power and strength. Usually skeletal muscles are attached to one end of a bone. They stretch across a joint and attach to the end of another bone.

Like all muscles, skeletal muscles work by contracting. When you bend your leg to kick a soccer ball, the skeletal muscles in the back of your thigh contract and they pull your leg bones up and back.

Some skeletal muscles are big, like the ones in your back that help to keep you standing straight and tall. Some skeletal muscles are smaller, like the ones in your neck that help you turn your head from side to side.

There are many skeletal muscles. There are almost too many to name. Some of the more important skeletal muscles you've probably heard of already.

Your shoulder muscles are called **deltoids** (DELL toydz). These muscles help you move your shoulders around and around.

Under your ribs are your **rectus abdominus** (RECK tuss ab DOM in uss) muscles. You've probably heard them called "abs." These muscles help you do sit-ups.

When you make a muscle with your arm, the muscle that you see push up under the skin of your upper arm is called your **biceps** (BYE seeps).

Tendons

Tendons (TEN dunz) help to hold skeletal muscles to bones. Tendons are tough cords, like ropes. They work like connector pieces between bones and muscles.

There are parts of your body that are small and are made up of very small bones, like your hands, fingers, feet and toes. Muscles wouldn't fit in these places. Specially shaped tendons extend all the way to the tips of your fingers and toes and connect the bones there to muscles higher up in your arms and legs. You really have no muscles in your fingers. You can move them because of tendons working together with muscles in your arms.

Taking Care of Your Muscles

Your muscles do very important things. They keep your heart beating and they let you move your body. Because they are so important, it's important to take care of them.

To keep your cardiac and skeletal muscles healthy and strong, you should try **aerobic** (air OH bick) exercise. Aerobic exercise is exercise that brings in oxygen to your skeletal muscles. Exercises like swimming, jogging, and roller blading are aerobic exercises. When you bring in more oxygen, your cardiac muscles become stronger and more powerful.

If you want to make your skeletal muscles bigger and stronger, try things like push-ups, crunches, pull-ups, and bike riding.

1. What do we call muscles that we can control ourselves?
2. What do we call muscles that we can **not** control ourselves?
3. Name the three types of muscles.
4. What kind of muscle is your heart?
5. What type of muscle surrounds the stomach and blood vessels?
6. The muscles that move your arms and legs are what type of muscle?
7. Which muscle group is **not** below your ribs?
8. What attaches muscles to bones?
9. Your muscles do what two important things?
10. Aerobic exercise helps strengthen which two types of muscles?

Part D - Bonus

The meanings of some word parts can help you understand the meanings of words that use those parts. The word **graph** comes from Greek and means to write or draw. Something **graphic** is written or drawn with a lot of detail.

Bio also comes from Greek. It means life. You see it in the word, **biology**.

When we put **bio** and **graph** together, it means something like write about a life. With the ending **y**, we get **biography**. A **biography** is a **nonfiction** story about someone's life. **Biography** is the bonus word for this lesson.

BONUS REVIEW

The opposite of **nonfiction** is **fiction**.

Some **pronouns** are: them, its, her, she, and us.

A **detail** is a small part of something. The chapter on muscles is **mostly about** muscles. There are many **details** in that chapter.

Lesson 37

Part A- Counting Pronouns

Directions: Read the story below. Count the number of times the pronouns *he*, *him*, and *his* are used to refer to Luke.

Everyone knows that Luke wants to be a nurse when he grows up. Luke tells all his friends and family about his plans to be a nurse. He even volunteers at the hospital every week. He volunteers so that he can see what nurses really do for patients. All the nurses at the hospital love him. They can see that he really cares about the health of each and every patient. Luke thinks he will be a good nurse. He thinks that because he enjoys his work at the hospital so much.

Total number of times that he, him, and his refer to Luke: _____
Note: this passage is **mostly about** Luke and what he wants to be when he grows up.

Part B- Vocabulary (Matching)

Directions: Find the definitions from the box that match the words below.

a.	space
b.	flag
c.	folds
d.	put on
e.	smart

Write the letter of the definition that matches each word.

1. creases _____

2. banner _____

3. intelligent _____

4. gap _____

5. donned _____

Part C- Review

Directions: Read the passage, and then answer the questions.

Most of the time the weather is something we enjoy. Other times, the weather can turn dangerous. Dangerous weather can cause problems like tornadoes, hurricanes, and floods. We call these things natural disasters. They are natural because they come from nature. They are disasters because they often cause many problems.

There are many different kinds of natural disasters: floods, hurricanes, tornadoes, volcanoes, earthquakes, wildfires, and winter storms. Different parts of the country see different kinds of natural disasters. Coastal areas are more likely to see hurricanes. People in flat, open places are more likely to have a tornado. Those who live by a river are more likely to have a flood.

One kind of natural disaster that you may never have heard of before is a tsunami (pronounced soo-nahm-ee). A tsunami is a group of huge waves. They happen when there is an earthquake or volcano under the sea. The huge waves can be as high as 100 feet. The waves can destroy everything in their path. People in Hawaii see tsunamis about once a year.

The worst part about natural disasters is that people are sometimes killed or hurt by them. Many times, natural disasters destroy houses and businesses. Some people have lost all their <u>possessions</u> in natural disasters.

1. According to the passage, what area of the country is most likely to experience hurricanes?

_____

2. How high can tsunamis be?

_____

3. What part of the country do you think is most likely to experience winter storms?

    a.   places that get lots of snow

    b.   places that stay warm in the winter

    c.   places where it never snows

    d.   the desert

4. Where do you think is the most dangerous place to be in a natural disaster?

    a.   in the basement

    b.   in a storm shelter

    c.   outside

5. In this passage, <u>possessions</u> means:

_____

6. Put an X next to each statement that is a small *detail* from the passage about natural disasters.

    1. _____ You can learn about a storm from watching the news.

    2. _____ Sometimes people get hurt in natural disasters.

    3. _____ A tornado is a natural disaster.

    4. _____ Tsunamis happen about once a year in Hawaii.

    5. _____ Hurricanes often hit areas along the coast.

Part D - Bonus

Remember, the word **graph** comes from Greek and means to write or draw. **Bio** also comes from Greek. It means life. When we add the ending **y**, we get **biography**. A **biography** is a **nonfiction** story about someone's life.

Auto is also from Greek. It means self. An **automobile** is like a wagon that runs by itself, without the help of a horse!

An **autobiography** is about the same as a **biography**, except the person who writes an **autobiography** writes about him*self* or her*self*. Like a **biography**, an **autobiography** is **nonfiction**.

BONUS REVIEW.

Some **pronouns** are: your, we, his, it, and their.

A **detail** is a small part of something.

When you answer an **inference** question, you have to use what you know, along with information in the passage.

Lesson 38

Part A- Parts of a Story

Directions: Read the passage, and then answer the question.

NOTE: This story has more than three parts.

Raquel's favorite part of school is her best friend Juan-Carlos. Raquel doesn't get to see Juan-Carlos much outside of school because he lives on the other side of town. Every day at recess you can see Raquel and Juan-Carlos playing four square. Those two are the four square champions of the school.

There are other times of the day Raquel and Juan-Carlos see each other as well. At 10:00 in the morning they have science class together. Science is their favorite subject because they are lab partners. That means that they get to do experiments together. After science Raquel has math class, but Juan-Carlos has French class. At noon they eat lunch together. Recess is after lunch, so they are together again.

In the afternoon, Juan-Carlos and Raquel only have one class together. They both have social studies at 2:00. After school they usually play some more four square before going home for homework and dinner. If they start to miss each other on the weekends, they call each other to talk. Raquel and Juan-Carlos are the closest friends in school.

science class		recess
1	2	3

1. Which of these belongs in Box 2? That is, which event happened *between* the thing in Box 1 and the thing in Box 3?

    a. phone call

    b. lunch

    c. social studies

    d. homework

Part B - Reading Subject Matter Books

Directions: Read the chapter on muscles, and then answer the questions at the end of the chapter.

Introduction

Your muscles are very important. Muscles do the same thing as a car engine. They turn energy into motion. Muscles move and make you capable of moving by **contracting** (cun TRAKT ing) and becoming shorter. Muscles pull, but they cannot push. Without your muscles you wouldn't be able to do most things. You wouldn't be able to play an instrument, throw a baseball, walk, talk or even smile. Your heart also wouldn't be able to pump blood through your body. People have over 650 muscles in our bodies. All of them have very important jobs to do.

Some muscles in our bodies work on their own, without us ever thinking about it. These muscles are called **involuntary** (in VOL un ter ee) muscles. Some muscles in our bodies we can control. These muscles are called **voluntary** (VOL un ter ee) muscles.

Muscles make up about half of your body weight. That means if you weigh 70 pounds, about 35 pounds of you is muscle. All muscles are made of the same thing. They are made of hundreds and thousands of small **elastic** (UH las tik) fibers.

People have three kinds of muscles: **cardiac** (CAR dee ak) muscles, smooth muscles, and **skeletal** (SKELL it ull) muscles.

Cardiac Muscles

Cardiac muscles are found only in the heart. They create the power that pumps blood through your body. Cardiac muscles contract to pump blood out of the heart. Then, they relax to let blood back into the heart.

Cardiac muscles are involuntary muscles. That means that your brain and nervous system tell the cardiac muscles what to do. They do it without you ever thinking about it. Think about how many times each day your cardiac muscles pump blood through your body without you ever thinking about it!

Smooth Muscles

You know that cardiac muscles are involuntary muscles. Smooth muscles are also involuntary muscles. They help our bodies in many different ways.

Smooth muscles surround or are part of your organs. Smooth muscles are in your stomach, helping you to **digest** (die JEST) food. They are in your bladder, helping you control when you urinate. They are in your blood **vessels** helping to deliver blood throughout your body. They are also in your airways, helping you breathe. Smooth muscles are found in many parts of your body helping your body do the things that keep you healthy every day.

Skeletal Muscles

Skeletal muscles are the kind of muscles most of us know about. They are the muscles that help us kick a soccer ball. Skeletal muscles are voluntary muscles. That means that they are muscles that we control. Your leg won't kick a soccer ball unless you want it to!

Working with your bones, skeletal muscles give you power and strength. Usually skeletal muscles are attached to one end of a bone. They stretch across a joint and attach to the end of another bone.

Like all muscles, skeletal muscles work by contracting. When you bend your leg to kick a soccer ball, the skeletal muscles in the back of your thigh contract and they pull your leg bones up and back.

Some skeletal muscles are big, like the ones in your back that help to keep you standing straight and tall. Some skeletal muscles are smaller, like the ones in your neck that help you turn your head from side to side.

There are many skeletal muscles. There are almost too many to name. Some of the more important skeletal muscles you've probably heard of already.

Your shoulder muscles are called **deltoids** (DELL toydz). These muscles help you move your shoulders around and around.

Under your ribs are your **rectus abdominus** (RECK tuss ab DOM in uss) muscles. You've probably heard them called "abs." These muscles help you do sit-ups.

When you make a muscle with your arm, the muscle that you see push up under the skin of your upper arm is called your **biceps** (BYE seeps).

Tendons

Tendons (TEN dunz) help to hold skeletal muscles to bones. Tendons are tough cords, like ropes. They work like connector pieces between bones and muscles.

There are parts of your body that are small and are made up of very small bones, like your hands, fingers, feet and toes. Muscles wouldn't fit in these places. Specially shaped tendons extend all the way to the tips of your fingers and toes and connect the bones there to muscles higher up in your arms and legs. You really have no muscles in your fingers. You can move them because of tendons working together with muscles in your arms.

Taking Care of Your Muscles

Your muscles do very important things. They keep your heart beating and they let you move your body. Because they are so important, it's important to take care of them.

To keep your cardiac and skeletal muscles healthy and strong, you should try **aerobic** (air OH bick) exercise. Aerobic exercise is exercise that brings in oxygen to your skeletal muscles. Exercises like swimming, jogging, and roller blading are aerobic exercises. When you bring in more oxygen, your cardiac muscles become stronger and more powerful.

If you want to make your skeletal muscles bigger and stronger, try things like push-ups, crunches, pull-ups, and bike riding.

1. What do we call muscles that we can control ourselves?

_____

2. What do we call muscles that we can **not** control ourselves?

_____

3. Name the three types of muscles.

_____

4. What kind of muscle is your heart?

_____

5. What type of muscle surrounds the stomach and blood vessels?

_____

6. The muscles that move your arms and legs are what type of muscle?

_____

7. Which muscle group is **not** below your ribs?

    a. abs

    b. abdominal

    c. deltoids

    d. abdominus rectus

8. What attaches muscles to bones?

_____

9. Your muscles do what two important things?

_____

10. Aerobic exercise helps strengthen which two types of muscles?

_____

Part C- Bonus

Remember, a **biography** is a **nonfiction** story about someone's life.

An **autobiography** is about the same as a **biography**, except the person who writes an **autobiography** writes about him*self* or her*self*. **Auto** is from Greek. It means self. Like a **biography**, an **autobiography** is **nonfiction**.

BONUS REVIEW.

Some **pronouns** are: she, hers, her, he, his, and him.

A **detail** is a small part of something.

When you answer an **inference** question, you use information from a passage, as well as knowledge you already have.

Lesson 39

Part A - Vocabulary

Directions: After you read each model, choose the word from the list that could *best* replace the underlined word in the model sentence.

1. **Model:** It started to rain when I was walking home from school. Because I didn't have an umbrella, my hair got <u>damp</u>.

    a.   blue

    b.   long

    c.   wet

    d.   straight

2. **Model:** I had a <u>horrible</u> day. I failed my math test, I scraped my knee during recess, and I missed my bus home.

    a.   very bad

    b.   very good

    c.   strange

    d.   happy

Part B- Vocabulary (Matching)

Directions: Find the definitions from the box that match the words below.

```
a.   smell

b.   deal

c.   damp

d.   smart

e.   long hole
```

Write the letter of the definition that matches each word.

1. wet _____

2. ditch _____

3. scent _____

4. bargain _____

5. intelligent _____

Part C- Review

Directions: Read the passage, and then answer the questions.

I think that it would be fun to be a chef. Mostly, I would like to be a pastry chef. The pastry chef is the person who makes all the desserts. I think the most fun would be to come up with dessert inventions. Right now my favorite dessert is chocolate chip cookies. My dad taught me how to make them.

To make chocolate chip cookies, you have to make sure you have all the ingredients. You need flour, sugar, brown sugar, eggs, chocolate chips, vanilla, salt, and baking soda. Before you start mixing, you should preheat the oven.

The sugars, egg, and vanilla get mixed together first. Then the flour, baking soda, and salt should be combined. After that, the flour mixture gets added to the sugar mixture. The last step of mixing is adding the chocolate chips. The best part is the actual baking. If your oven has a light inside, you can watch the cookies bake.

My father says that baking cookies is his favorite <u>scent</u>. Chocolate chips cookies are not his favorite cookies, though. His favorite are peanut butter cookies. My dad loves cookies, and he is very good at making them. The whole family says no one makes peanut butter cookies like he does. My dad usually ends up eating most of his own cookies. Sometimes it only takes him two days to eat the whole batch!

1. According to the passage, what does a pastry chef do?

_____

2. What is the author's favorite dessert?

_____

3. Is this passage fiction or nonfiction?

_____

4. Why do you think you need to preheat the oven?

    a.   so that the cookies don't get eaten

    b.   so that it is clean

    c.   so that the oven can rest

    d.   so it is hot when you put the cookies in to bake

5. What do you think you need to do to the eggs before mixing them with the sugar and vanilla?

    a.   color them

    b.   break them

    c.   wash them

    d.   cook them

6. Look at the last paragraph of the passage. Count how many times the pronouns *he*, *him*, or *his* are used to refer to my dad.

_____

7. In this passage, <u>scent</u> means:

_____

8. Which belongs in box 2 below?

preheat oven		bake
1	2	3

    a.   eat cookies

    b.   watch cookies bake

    c.   mix ingredients

9. Put an X next to each statement that is a small *detail* from the passage about making chocolate chip cookies.

1. _____ Pastry chefs make desserts.
2. _____ Chocolate chip is the author's favorite dessert.
3. _____ Oatmeal cookies are good too.
4. _____ Peanut butter is the author's dad's favorite cookie.
5. _____ When making cookies, you should preheat the oven.

Part D - Bonus

Remember, a **biography** is a **nonfiction** story about someone's life.

Remember, **auto** is from Greek. It means self. A **biography** written by the person who the book is about is called an **autobiography**. Both are **nonfiction**.

BONUS REVIEW

Passages are **mostly about** something. Passages have many **details** about whatever the passage is **mostly about**.

When you answer an **inference** question, you use information from a passage, as well as knowledge you already have.

Lesson 41

Part A- What Will Happen Next

Directions: Read the passage, and then answer the questions.

Our teacher had told us a thousand times that we would lose points if we turned in our projects late. The night before the projects were due, I set mine out on the kitchen counter. I leave for school through the door in the kitchen, so I figured I couldn't possibly forget my project.

Just as I was about to leave for school, the phone rang. It was my best friend, Marshall. He was very upset. He thought he might have left part of his project in our car. He and I had worked on our projects together the day before. My dad drove him home after that. Marshall wanted me to run out to the car to see if part of his project was there.

I had a remote phone, so I went out to the car to look. My mom was already in the car, waiting to take me to school. Fortunately, Marshall's project was in the car. As my mom told me to hurry up, I lay down the phone in the garage.

What will probably happen next?

Hint: Each answer *could* happen next. The question asks what will *probably* happen next. This is an inference question. You have to decide what is *most likely* to happen next.

    a.   The person telling the story will return to the house to get her project.

    b.   The person telling the story will jump in the car and drive off to school without her own project.

    c.   The person's mom will tell the person telling the story to go back in the house and get the project.

    d.   The person telling the story will remember the project, but will leave it home on purpose in order to get to school on time.

Part B- Vocabulary

Directions: Find the definitions from the box that match the words below.

a.	things you own
b.	smell
c.	try
d.	fight
e.	short

Write the letter of the definition that matches each word.

1. argue _____

2. brief _____

3. possessions _____

4. scent _____

5. attempt _____

Part C- Reading Subject Matter Books

Directions: Read the information below from a science book, and then follow your teacher's instructions.

Name of Book: General Science Today

Table of Contents:

Unit 1...............Classification of Animals

Unit 2...............The Human Body

    Chapter 1: The Muscle System

    Chapter 2: The Skeletal System

        Introduction

        The Spine

        The Ribs

        Hands

        The Skull

        Legs

        Joints

        Taking Care of your Bones

    Chapter 3: The Nervous System

    Chapter 4: Vision

    Chapter 5: Hearing

Unit 3...............Light and Optics

Unit 4...............Sound

Unit 5...............Ecology

Unit 6...............Astronomy

1. What is Unit 2, Chapter 2 probably about?

2. What is the human spine?

3. Do you think bones are dead or living, and why do you think so?

4. What are the names of some human bones?

5. What do you already know about bones?

Part D- Review

Directions: Read the passage, and then answer the questions.

Have you ever wondered why leaves change color in the fall? You may have noticed that some trees are always green. These trees are called evergreen trees. They stay green throughout all the seasons. The trees that change color in the fall are called deciduous (duh-SID-you-us) trees.

You may know that trees need sunlight to make food. They use a chemical called chlorophyll (KLOR-o-fil) to make their food. Chlorophyll causes the tree's leaves to look green. In the fall, the days get shorter and trees get less sunshine. Because they only get a brief amount of sun, trees stop making chlorophyll. The other colors in the leaves that were covered up by the green chlorophyll come out.

Some years the colors of the leaves are brighter and prettier than others. If the weather in early fall is cool but not freezing, the leaves turn brighter colors. Also, if there is only a small amount of rain, the leaves are brighter.

You also know that deciduous trees lose their leaves in the fall. After the leaves change color, they drop to the ground. These trees are preparing for winter. You can think of the trees as hibernating for the winter months. In the spring, new leaves will grow in the place of the fallen leaves.

1. According to the passage, what chemical helps trees make their own food?

_____

2. What are trees that stay green throughout the whole year called?

_____

3. Is this passage fiction or nonfiction?

_____

4. Why do you think deciduous trees drop their leaves in the fall?

   a. there is not enough sun in the winter for the leaves to make food

   b. no one likes to look at trees in the winter

   c. the leaves would get in the way of snow falling

   d. trees die each fall

5. Why do you think the fall colors are less bright when there is a lot of rain?

   a. the trees don't know that winter is coming

   b. the trees get depressed

   c. the leaves don't get the sunshine they need to change color

   d. the trees want the leaves to protect them from the rain

6. Look at the second paragraph of the passage. Count how many times pronouns are used to refer to trees.

_____

7. In this passage, brief means:

_____

8. Which belongs in box 2 below?

days get shorter		color of leaves changes
1	2	3

   a. it rains

   b. there is less sunshine

   c. it is cold

9. Put an X next to each statement that is a small *detail* from the passage about leaves changing color in the fall.

1. _____ There are two kinds of trees.
2. _____ Trees need chlorophyll to make food.
3. _____ The days get shorter in the fall.
4. _____ Deciduous trees lose their leaves in the fall.
5. _____ Autumn is another name for fall.

Part E- Bonus

You probably know how to **classify** things. For example, the following items belong in one **class** of things:

cars, airplanes, trains, trucks, boats, motorcycles

To **classify**, you must decide what all of those things have in common. In this case, all of the things belong to the **class** of "types of transportation."

Many times, being able to **classify** well helps you better understand what you read. **Classifying** also helps you when you write.

BONUS REVIEW

You know that **fiction** comes from the imagination of a writer. When writing is true or factual, it is called **nonfiction**.

Remember that all the words below are **pronouns**:

I	me	my
you	him	your
it	us	its
she	their	her
he	they	his
we	them	our

A **biography** written by the person who the book is about is called an **autobiography**. Both **biography** and **autobiography** are **nonfiction**.

Lesson 42

Part A - What Will Happen Next

Directions: Read the passage, and then answer the questions.

I had begged my parents for a dog. My parents always told me, "Maybe someday." Then one day, my teacher planned a field trip to our local animal shelter. I asked my mom to go on the trip with my class. I thought if she saw the dogs, she would fall in love with one.

My mom said she would come on the trip. I was so excited. The night before the trip, I couldn't even fall asleep. I knew that when she saw those dogs, she would let me get one.

The day of the trip, we got to the shelter right on time. There were dogs everywhere! My mom walked in and went right over to a tiny brown puppy. When she picked him up, he started licking her nose. She was laughing and cuddling with the puppy.

What will probably happen next?

Hint: Each answer *could* happen next. The question asks what will *probably* happen next. This is an inference question. You have to decide what is *most likely* to happen next.

    a.   they will go home with the tiny brown puppy

    b.   the mom will say they still can't get a dog

    c.   they will get a different dog from the shelter

Part B- Classification

Directions: After reading the lists below, classify the items in the lists.

1. got in the car
   drove to a state park
   found a place to put up the tent
   built a camp fire
   did some fishing
   went hiking on a nature trail
   These are all things someone might do when:

   a. going hunting

   b. going to a hotel for a vacation

   c. camping

   d. fishing

2. make the bed
   wash the dishes
   clean up your bedroom
   put out the garbage
   vacuum the rug in the living room
   These are all types of:

   a. homework

   b. household chores

   c. cleaning

   d. things in the living room

3. hit the ball with a bat
   catch the ball
   throw the ball
   pitch
   run bases
   These are all things related to:

   a. playing baseball

   b. playing with balls

   c. football

   d. P.E. class

Part C- Reading Subject Matter Books-Word Pronunciation

Directions: Below are some vocabulary words from a book chapter about the skeletal system. Your teacher will read each word for you and then will ask you to pronounce it.

1. **minerals** (MIN er uls)

2. **calcium** (CAL see um)

3. **skull** (skul)

4. **jaw** (jaw)

5. **stirrup** (STIR up)

6. **vertebra** (VER tuh bruh)

7. **spinal cord** (SPY nul kord)

8. **vertebrae** (VER tuh bray)

9. **organs** (OR guns)

10. **sternum** (STIR num)

Part D - Bonus

Here are some details from a paragraph you read in Lesson 41:

    trees need sunlight to make food
    trees use chlorophyll (KLOR-o-fil) to make their food
    chlorophyll causes the tree's leaves to look green
    trees get less sunshine in the fall
    trees stop making chlorophyll when they don't get sun
    the other colors in the leaves come out in the fall

We can **classify** these details. That is, we can see how all the **details** are related to one topic: leaves changing color in the fall.

BONUS REVIEW

When you **classify details**, that helps you find out what a passage is **mostly about**.

Lesson 43

Part A- Vocabulary

Directions: Find the definitions from the box that match the words below.

a.	skin
b.	leave out
c.	writer
d.	laugh
e.	round

Write the letter of the definition that matches each word.

1. omit _____

2. flesh _____

3. giggle _____

4. circular _____

5. author _____

Part B- Reading Subject Matter Books-Word Pronunciation

Directions: Below are some vocabulary words from a book chapter about the skeletal system.
Your teacher will read each word for you and then will ask you to pronounce it.

1. **radius** (RAY dee us)

2. **ulna** (UL nuh)

3. **humerus** (HYOU mer us)

4. **pelvis** (PELL vus)

5. **femur** (FEE mer)

6. **tibia** (TIB ee uh)

7. **fibula** (FIB you luh)

8. **patella** (PAH tell uh)

9. **joint** (JOYNT)

10. **socket** (SOCK ut)

11. **ligaments** (LIG uh ments)

Part C- Classification

Directions: After reading the lists below, classify the items in the lists.

1. got a ball
   went to the park
   met some friends
   started a game
   played for two hours
   everyone made several baskets
   These are all things someone might do when:

   a. making baskets from straw

   b. playing in your yard

   c. at school

   d. playing basketball

2. sit at a desk
    read books
    take tests
    raise your hand
    listen to the teacher
    These are things you might do:

    a.   at a camp

    b.   at home

    c.   in school

    d.   when you exercise

3. sit down
    play several scales
    play some songs
    play each song four or five times
    These are all things related to:

    a.   practicing a musical instrument

    b.   singing

    c.   preforming with a band

    d.   listening to music

Part D- Review

Directions: Read the passage, and then answer the questions.

Years before English settlers arrived in Jamestown, there was another colony of English settlers. It was the Roanoke colony in what is now North Carolina. What happened to these settlers has always been a mystery.

Roanoke was first spotted by English explorers in 1584. They thought that it would be a good place to have a colony. The next year, Queen Elizabeth sent 100 men to live on Roanoke. The settlers built a fort and houses, but they had some troubles. They were not able to plant enough food. They also began to <u>argue</u> with the native Roanoke Indian tribe.

In 1586 Sir Francis Drake sailed past Roanoke. The Roanoke settlers were so miserable that they asked Drake to take them back to England. The next year, 150 men, women, and children from England were sent to live in Roanoke. During the first year, Virginia Dare was born. She was the first English settler born in the New World. Some people call her the first American.

The new settlers also argued with the Native Americans in the area. But, they grew crops and continued to live in Roanoke. The settlers did not have any visitors from England for two years. In 1590, an English ship with supplies for the colony arrived in Roanoke. What they found was a completely empty island. There was no sign of the colonists. To this day, no one knows what happened to the Roanoke colonists.

1. According to the passage, what country were the Roanoke settlers from?

    _____

2. When was Roanoke first spotted by English explorers?

    _____

3. Is this passage fiction or nonfiction?

    _____

4. Why do you think the first settlers wanted to leave Roanoke to go back to England?

    a.   they didn't like the weather in America

    b.   they didn't have enough food

    c.   they didn't know how to speak English

    d.   they were bored

5. Why do you think that people wanted to settle in Roanoke?

    a.   they thought that they could start a new community in America

    b.   they didn't have any friends in England

    c.   they thought that the land was better in America

    d.   they thought that the food was better in America

6. Look at the third paragraph of the passage. Count how many times pronouns are used to refer to Virginia Dare.

_____

7. In this passage, <u>argue</u> means:

_____

8. Which belongs in box 1 below?

	100 men sent to live in Roanoke	150 men, women, and children sent to live in Roanoke
1	2	3

    a.   settlers disappear

    b.   settlers argue with the indians on Roanoke

    c.   explorers see Roanoke for the first time

9. Put an X next to each statement that is a small *detail* from the passage about the Roanoke colony.

   1. _____ The settlers planted squash.

   2. _____ Some people refer to Virginia Dare as the first American.

   3. _____ The first Roanoke settlers built a fort.

   4. _____ The first Roanoke settlers wanted to go back to England.

   5. _____ An English ship returned to Roanoke in 1590.

Part E - Bonus

Here are some details from a paragraph you read in Part D of this lesson:

    Roanoke settlers argued with Native Americans

    grew crops and stayed in area

    had no visitors from England for two years

    English ship arrived in 1590

    found no colonists

    no one knows what happened to colonists

We can **classify** these details. That is, we can see how all the **details** are related to one topic: the Roanoke colony.

BONUS REVIEW

When you **classify details**, that helps you find out what a passage is **mostly about**.

Lesson 44

Part A - What Will Happen Next

Directions: Read the passage, and then answer the questions.

Anna was a great swimmer. She had been swimming since she was four years old. She was the fastest swimmer on the team at her high school. There was no one on the team who even came close to catching her. The star swimmer from the town next door had come close to beating Anna once. But Anna had won that race. They were going to race each other again on Saturday.

The week before the race, Anna practiced every day. She woke up early and went to the pool. She also went to the pool after school. She practiced for three hours every day that week. On Friday night, Anna swam the distance of the race faster than she ever had before.

Anna got a good night's sleep on Friday night. On Saturday morning, she had a good breakfast and went to the race. She got in the pool to warm up. She had never felt better.

What will probably happen next?

Hint: Each answer *could* happen next. The question asks what will *probably* happen next. This is an inference question. You have to decide what is *most likely* to happen next.

a. Anna will lose the race.

b. There will be a tie.

c. Anna will get hurt and won't be able to race.

d. Anna will win the race.

Part B- Classification

Directions: After reading the list below, classify the items in the list.

1. drop cloth
   brushes
   turpentine
   cans of paint
   ladder
   These are all things you might use if you were:

   a. working outside

   b. cleaning the house

   c. painting a model

   d. painting a room in a house

2. brushed my teeth
   changed into pajamas
   read in bed
   went to sleep
   These are all things someone might do when he or she is:

   a. going to bed

   b. getting up in the morning

   c. getting ready for school

   d. getting ready for a party

3. parked the car
    walked to the mall
    bought some jeans at one store
    bought a jacket at another store
    looked at T-shirts at a third store
    had something to eat
    went back to the car
    These are all things someone might do when he or she is:

    a.   going out to dinner

    b.   taking driving lessons

    c.   shopping

    d.   going on vacation

Part C- Reading Subject Matter Books

Directions: Below is all of Chapter 2 from Unit 2 of the book, *General Science Today*. You are not going to read the whole chapter in today's lesson.

Instead, you are just going to read _the first paragraph_ after each heading. After you read the first paragraph after a heading, answer the questions for that paragraph.

The first paragraph and the questions for that paragraph are in boxes.

Introduction

The 206 bones in our bodies have important purposes. Our organs and other tissues are attached to our bones. Bones protect organs such as the heart, the brain, and the lungs. Some of our bones make blood cells. Finally, bones store **minerals** (MIN er uls) that we need, such as **calcium** (CAL see um).

1. How many bones do we have in our body?

   _____

2. Which job do bones **not** do?

   a. protect organs

   b. help us breathe

   c. make blood cells

   d. store minerals

3. What parts of our bodies are attached to our bones?

   _____

The Skull

The bones in your head are referred to as your **skull** (skul). Most of those bones protect your brain. The bones you can feel at the top of your head, in the back, and on the sides are the ones that protect your brain.

4. Which organ does your skull protect?

   a. heart

   b. brain

   c. lungs

Other bones in the skull make up your face. Under your eyes, you can feel the holes in the bones where your eyes are. The only bone in your head that moves is your lower **jaw** (jaw). That bone makes it possible for you to chew food and to open and close your mouth.

The smallest bone in your whole body is in your head. That is the **stirrup** (STIR up) bone, which is right behind your eardrum. That tiny bone is only about 1/10 of an inch long.

The Spine

Another name for your spine is "backbone." There are really 25 different bones that make up our backbones. Each bone is called a **vertebra** (VER tuh bruh). When you touch the middle of your back, you can feel some of those bones.

5. What is another name for the spine?

_____

Our spines help us to stand up straight. They also let us twist and bend. The most important job of the backbone is to protect the **spinal cord** (SPY nul kord). The spinal cord is made from many nerves. Nerves send messages between your brain and the rest of your body. The spinal cord goes right down the middle of the bones in the spine. The **vertebrae** (VER tuh bray; plural for vertebra) have small pads between them. The pads are like pillows between each vertebra. They keep the vertebrae from rubbing against each other.

The Ribs

Your ribs are like a cage. They protect special **organs** (OR guns) in your body. The most important organs that the ribs protect are your heart, your lungs, and your liver.

6. What are the most important organs that the ribs protect?

    _____

7. What are the ribs like?

    a.   a cage

    b.   a pump

    c.   ropes

You can feel your ribs along the sides and front of your chest. When you take a deep breath, you can see the ribs in your chest. You have one set of ribs in the front and one in back. Most people have 12 pairs of ribs. They are all attached to the vertebra in your spine. Some of them attach to the **sternum** (STIR num). The sternum is a hard bone in the middle of your chest.

Hands and Arms

There are three bones in each of your arms. There are *fifty-four* bones in the wrists and hands. That includes all the bones in your fingers. Those bones don't protect organs like the ribs do. They let you do many activities, though. It is not even possible to name them all. When you type, play a sport, swing on a swing, or scratch your head, you're using your arms, wrists, and hands.

8. Do the wrist and hand bones protect organs?

_____

9. How many bones are there in the wrists and hands?

    a. 24

    b. 3

    c. 54

Your arm has two big bones between your elbow and your hand. They are called the **radius** (RAY dee us) and the **ulna** (UL nuh). There is just one big bone between your shoulder and your elbow. It is called the **humerus** (HYOU mer us). Eight small bones at the end of the radius and ulna make up your wrist. The middle part of each hand has five bones. There are two bones in each thumb. There are three bones in each finger. All those bones in your wrist, hands, and fingers are able to move.

Legs and Feet

Your leg bones are large. They have to be big because they support the weight of your whole body. The biggest bones in your body are between your **pelvis** (PELL vus) and your knees. That bone is called a **femur** (FEE mer). The tops of the femurs are attached to the pelvis. The pelvis bones are shaped like a circle. The pelvis holds up your spine. It also protects some parts of your digestive system and other organs.

10. Why are your leg bones large?

_____

11. What is the bone between your pelvis and knee called?

_____

You have two more bones in the bottom part of each leg. They are called the **tibia** (TIB ee uh) and the **fibula** (FIB you luh). Your ankles and feet are attached to those bones. There are seven bones in your ankle. Each foot has five bones. Your big toes have two bones each. The rest of your toes have three small bones each. The total number of bones in both feet, ankles, and toes, is 52.

We can't forget about your kneecap. The name of that bone is the **patella** (PAH tell uh). That bone is shaped like a triangle. It protects the knee joint.

You couldn't stand up, walk, run, or jump without all the bones in your legs, ankles, feet, and toes. The shape of your feet helps you stand up straight and keep your balance.

Moving Joints

The area where two bones meet is called a **joint** (JOYNT). Many of our joints move. That is what helps us move. Some joints work just like a door. You can close your arm and open it, like closing and opening a door. Most doors open and close in just one direction. Your arms and legs open and close in just one direction too.

12. What do joints do?

_____

The joints in your shoulders and hips are different. Those joints have a ball inside a **socket** (SOCK ut). That kind of joint lets you move your shoulders and hips in many directions.

The bones in your joints don't rub against each other. They are attached to each other with **ligaments** (LIG uh ments). Ligaments are very strong and flexible. They also help hold some organs in place. Your joints have a kind of liquid in them that helps the bones move smoothly. That is a lot like putting oil on a door to make it open and close better.

Taking Care of Your Bones

Your bones protect you and help you. You should take care of them. One way of taking care of your bones is to eat and drink foods that are good for you. Food helps you grow strong, healthy bones. Milk, low-fat cheese, yogurt, and ice cream have all the calcium your bones need. Most people don't mind eating ice cream to make their bones strong.

13. Name two foods that give your body calcium?

_____

The other way to take care of your bones is to protect them. You should wear the right protection for different kinds of sports and activities. When you play football or hockey you need a helmet and pads for protection. Remember how your skull protects your brain? You should help out by always wearing a helmet when you ride a bike. If you ride a skateboard or scooter, you should also wear pads.

Part D Bonus

Here are some details from a paragraph you have been reading in the chapter on skeletons:

  two bones in each lower leg
  ankles and feet attached to them
  seven bones in each ankle
  eight bones in each foot
  two bones in each big toe
  three small bones in other toes

We can **classify** these details. That is, we can see how all the **details** are related to one topic: many bones in our feet.

BONUS REVIEW

When you **classify details**, that helps you find out what a passage is **mostly about**.

Remember, a **biography** is a **nonfiction** story about someone's life.

Fiction comes from the imagination of the writer. When there are things in a story that couldn't possibly be true, you know the story is **fiction**.

Lesson 46

Part A- Vocabulary

Directions: After you read each model, choose the word from the list that could *best* replace the underlined word in the model sentence.

1. **Model:** There has always been an empty lot next to my apartment building. Last week someone bought it and they are going to <u>construct</u> an office building on the lot.

   a. tear down

   b. build

   c. fix

   d. own

2. **Model:** My uncle had to have heart surgery last week. He is feeling much better and the doctor says he will be <u>released</u> from the hospital next week. We'll be happy to have him home.

   a. let go

   b. kicked out

   c. billed

   d. moved

Part B- Classification

Directions: After reading the lists below, classify the items in the lists.

1. classical
   rock
   jazz
   rap
   country
   These are all types of:

   a. sports

   b. music

   c. careers

   d. people

2. peanut butter and jelly
    ham and cheese
    roast beef
    turkey
    grilled cheese
    These are all types of:

    a. restaurants

    b. fruits

    c. sandwiches

    d. breakfast foods

3. painting
    building models
    playing baseball
    collecting stamps
    dancing
    These are all types of:

    a. hobbies

    b. feelings

    c. schools

    d. chores

Part C- Review

Directions: Read the passage, and then answer the questions.

Have you every heard of Copernicus? Can you even say his name? It's pronounced: kuh-PER-ni-kuss. You've never met him. You may not know his name. But he came up with the greatest scientific theory in history.

He was many things. He was a mathematician. He was a governor. He was a doctor. And he was an <u>astronomer</u>. It was as an astronomer that Copernicus made his mark.

Before Copernicus, people thought the earth was the center of the universe. They also thought that the earth didn't rotate. People thought the sun moved around the earth. People also thought the other planets moved around the earth too. In fact, people thought everything moved around the earth. Copernicus studied the sun, planets, and stars for years. Then he came up with a theory. Copernicus said it was the sun that was at the center of everything.

Copernicus said that the earth rotating caused day and night. And he said that the earth orbiting the sun caused the seasons. He thought a rotating earth orbiting the sun made more sense than the whole universe orbiting the earth. He was right! Now everyone understands that the earth rotates causing day and night. And we also know that the earth and other planets orbit the sun.

He came up with his theory in the early 1500's. But his theory wasn't published until 1543, the year he died. He came up with it without even using a telescope. The telescope wasn't invented for another 100 years! Now that's impressive.

1. According to the passage, when did Copernicus come up with his theory?

    _____

2. Did Copernicus use a telescope in coming up with his theory?

    _____

3. This passage tells facts about a real person's life. Is it fiction or nonfiction?

    _____

4. Why do you think Copernicus came up with his theory?

    a. because he was bored

    b. because he didn't think the old theory was correct

    c. because he wanted to be famous

    d. because he liked disagreeing with people

5. In this passage, <u>astronomer</u> means:

    _____

6. Which belongs in box 2 below?

people thought sun orbited Earth		Copernicus came up with theory
1	2	3

   a. telescope is invented

   b. Copernicus published theory

   c. Copernicus studied sun, planets, and stars

Part D- Bonus

A **limerick** is a type of poem. **Limericks** are supposed to be funny, like a joke or a funny story. All **limericks** follow the same pattern. They all have five lines and have the same rhyme pattern.

Here is a **limerick** written by Edward Lear:

> There was a young lady whose chin,
>
> Resembled the point of a pin;
>
> So she had it made sharp,
>
> And purchased a harp,
>
> And played several tunes with her chin.

BONUS REVIEW

You know that **fiction** comes from the imagination of a writer. When writing is true or factual, it is called **nonfiction**.

Remember that all the words below are **pronouns**:

I	me	my
you	him	your
it	us	its
she	their	her
he	they	his
we	them	our

Lesson 47

Part A- Vocabulary

Directions: Find the definitions from the box that match the words below.

a.	buy
b.	build
c.	flag
d.	very loud
e.	let go

Write the letter of the definition that matches each word.

1. construct _____

2. purchase _____

3. release _____

4. deafening _____

5. banner _____

Part B- Classification

Directions: After reading the lists below, classify the items in the lists.

1. cake
   balloons
   games
   presents
   candles
   These are all things you would need if you were:

   a. going to school

   b. going on vacation

   c. baby sitting

   d. having a birthday party

2. paper
   pencils
   notebooks
   books
   book bag
   These are all things that you might:

   a. take to the pool

   b. take to school

   c. take to visit your grandmother

   d. take to soccer practice

3. go to the locker room
   put on a bathing suit
   bring a towel
   wear goggles
   wait for the teacher
   These are all things you might do if you were:

   a. taking swimming lessons

   b. going to the beach

   c. going to a baseball game

   d. taking gymnastics lessons

Part C - Reading Subject Matter Books

When you read a chapter from a book, you should read the questions at the end of the chapter *before* you read the chapter. That helps you focus on the most important parts of the chapter.

In this lesson, you're going to read the questions at the end of the science chapter on bones. You aren't going to read the passage in this lesson, and you aren't going to answer the questions. You're just going to read the questions and then try to remember as many of them as you can.

Part D- Reading Subject Matter Books (Continued)

Directions: Read the questions below from the end of the science chapter on bones, and then close your workbook.

1. What is another name for the backbone?
2. What is a vertebra?
3. What do your ribs **not** protect?
4. There are 54 bones in your:
5. Do the bones in your arms, wrists, hands, and fingers protect any organs?
6. What is the name of the bone between your pelvis and your knee?
7. What does your pelvis **not** do?
8. Name a part of your body that has a joint that moves like the hinge in a door.

9. What do your bones need that you can get by eating yogurt and other dairy products?

Part E- Review

Directions: Read the passage, and then answer the questions.

In my school, kids learn about the solar system in fifth grade. I am in fifth grade, so I studied the solar system this year. We learned facts about all the planets, plus the sun. Each planet is different. Some of the planets have rings, and some of them have moons.

Part of my final project was to build a model of the solar system. I had a model of all eight planets. The planets that have rings even had rings on them in my model. The person who loved my model the most was my little sister Olivia. She is in third grade. She has not studied the planets yet. Olivia is always interested in what I am doing in school. My father says that is because Olivia looks up to me. She wants to grow up to be like me.

My parents were excited that Olivia was so interested in the solar system. They even think that she might want to become an astronaut some day. Olivia will not study the solar system in school for another two years. My dad asked me if I would teach her what I know about the planets. Since then, I have taught her everything I learned, but she still wants to know more!

1. According to the passage, in what grade do kids get to study the solar system?

   _____

2. What was the author's final project?

   _____

3. How do you think the author feels about the fact that his little sister looks up to him?

   a. annoyed

   b. jealous

   c. proud

   d. sad

4. Look at the third paragraph of the passage. Count how many times pronouns are used to refer to Olivia.

   _____

5. Which belongs in box 3 below?

studied the solar system	made a model of the solar system	
1	2	3

    a.   made rings around the planets that have rings

    b.   taught Olivia about the solar system

    c.   started fifth grade

6. What do you think would be the best way for Olivia to learn more about the solar system?

    a.   the local library

    b.   her class at school

    c.   her parents

    d.   study her brother's model

Part F- Bonus

Limericks are funny poems. All **limericks** have five lines and the same rhythm pattern.

The rhythm pattern in lines 1 and 2 usually sounds like this: da DUM da da DUM da da DUM da. Lines 3 and 4 sound like this: da da DUM da da DUM. Line 5 sounds like this: da da DUM da da DUM da da DUM da. See if you can hear the rhythm pattern in the **limerick** by Edward Lear below:

There was   an old person   of   Dover,
da   DUM da da DUM da da DUM da

Who rushed through a field   of   blue clover;
da DUM da   da DUM da da DUM da

But some very   large bees,
da da   DUM da da   DUM

Stung his nose and his knees,
da da DUM da   da DUM

So he very   soon went   back to Dover.

da da DUM da   da   DUM   da   da   DUM da

BONUS REVIEW

When you **classify details**, that helps you find out what a passage is **mostly about**.

Lesson 48

Part A- Classification

Directions: After reading the lists below, classify the items in the lists.

1. checked the listing
    drove to the theatre
    bought a ticket
    bought popcorn
    found a seat
    These are all things you would do if you were:

    a. watching television

    b. seeing a movie

    c. playing a video game

    d. going to the mall

2. bread
    knife
    peanut butter
    jelly
    plate
    These are all things that you might need to:

    a. clean your room

    b. make cookies

    c. make a sandwich

    d. do your homework

3. collar
   leash
   food
   toys
   water dish

   These are all things you might need if you were:

   a.   getting a new puppy

   b.   getting a new brother or sister

   c.   playing basketball

   d.   getting a goldfish

Part B - Reading Subject Matter Books

Directions: You are going to read the chapter below on bones. First, however, look at the questions at the end of the chapter. Then read the chapter.

In another lesson, you will actually answer the questions at the end of the chapter.

Introduction

The 206 bones in our bodies have important purposes. Our organs and other tissues are attached to our bones. Bones protect organs such as the heart, the brain, and the lungs. Some of our bones make blood cells. Finally, bones store **minerals** (MIN er uls) that we need, such as **calcium** (CAL see um).

The Skull

The bones in your head are referred to as your **skull** (skul). Most of those bones protect your brain. The bones you can feel at the top of your head, in the back, and on the sides are the ones that protect your brain.

Other bones in the skull make up your face. Under your eyes, you can feel the holes in the bones where your eyes are. The only bone in your head that moves is your lower **jaw** (jaw). That bone makes it possible for you to chew food and to open and close your mouth.

The smallest bone in your whole body is in your head. That is the **stirrup** (STIR up) bone, which is right behind your eardrum. That tiny bone is only about 1/10 of an inch long.

The Spine

Another name for your spine is "backbone." There are really 25 different bones that make up our backbones. Each bone is called a **vertebra** (VER tuh bruh). When you touch the middle of your back you can feel some of those bones.

Our spines help us to stand up straight. They also let us twist and bend. The most important job of the backbone is to protect the **spinal cord** (SPY nul kord). The spinal cord is made from many nerves. Nerves send messages between your brain and the rest of your body. The spinal cord goes right down the middle of the bones in the spine. The **vertebrae** (VER tuh bray; plural for vertebra) have small pads between them. The pads are like pillows between each vertebra. They keep the vertebrae from rubbing against each other.

The Ribs

Your ribs are like a cage. They protect special organs (OR guns) in your body. The most important organs that the ribs protect are your heart, your lungs, and your liver.

You can feel your ribs along the sides and front of your chest. When you take a deep breath, you can see the ribs in your chest. You have one set of ribs in the front and one in the back. Most people have 12 pairs of ribs. They are all attached to the vertebra in your spine. Some of them attach to the **sternum** (STIR num). The sternum is a hard bone in the middle of your chest.

Hands and Arms

There are three bones in each of your arms. There are *fifty-four* bones in the wrists and hands. That includes all the bones in your fingers. Those bones don't protect organs like the ribs do. They let you do many activities, though. It is not even possible to name them all.

When you type, play a sport, swing on a swing, or scratch your head, you're using your arms, wrists, and hands.

Your arm has two big bones between your elbow and your hand. They are called the **radius** (RAY dee us) and the **ulna** (UL nuh). There is just one big bone between your shoulder and your elbow. It is called the **humerus** (HYOU mer us). Eight small bones at the end of the radius and ulna make up your wrist. The middle part of each hand has five bones. There are two bones in each thumb. There are three bones in each finger. All those bones in your wrist, hands, and fingers are able to move.

Legs and Feet

Your leg bones are large. They have to be big because they support the weight of your whole body. The biggest bones in your body are between your **pelvis** (PELL vus) and your knees. That bone is called a **femur** (FEE mer). The tops of the femurs are attached to the pelvis. The pelvis bones are shaped like a circle. The pelvis holds up your spine. It also protects some parts of your digestive system and other organs.

You have two more bones in the bottom part of each leg. They are called the **tibia** (TIB ee uh) and the **fibula** (FIB you luh). Your ankles and feet are attached to those bones. There are seven bones in your ankle. Each foot has five bones. Your big toes have two bones each. The rest of your toes have three small bones each. The total number of bones in both feet, ankles, and toes, is 52.

We can't forget about your kneecap. The name of that bone is the **patella** (PAH tell uh). That bone is shaped like a triangle. It protects the knee joint.

You couldn't stand up, walk, run, or jump without all the bones in your legs, ankles, feet, and toes. The shape of your feet helps you stand up straight and keep your balance.

Moving Joints

The area where two bones meet is called a **joint** (JOYNT). Many of our joints move. That is what helps us move. Some joints work just like a door. You can close your arm and open it, like closing and opening a door. Most doors open and close in just one direction. Your arms and legs open and close in just one direction too.

The joints in your shoulders and hips are different. Those joints have a ball inside a **socket** (SOCK ut). That kind of joint lets you move your shoulders and hips in many directions.

The bones in your joints don't rub against each other. They are attached to each other with **ligaments** (LIG uh ments). Ligaments are very strong and flexible. They also help hold some organs in place. Your joints have a kind of liquid in them that helps the bones move smoothly. That is a lot like putting oil on a door to make it open and close better.

Taking Care of Your Bones

Your bones protect you and help you. You should take care of them. One way of taking care of your bones is to eat and drink foods that are good for you. Food helps you grow strong, healthy bones. Milk, low-fat cheese, yogurt, and ice cream have all the calcium your bones need. Most people don't mind eating ice cream to make their bones strong.

The other way to take care of your bones is to protect them. You should wear the right protection for different kinds of sports and activities. When you play football or hockey you need a helmet and pads for protection. Remember how your skull protects your brain? You should help out by always wearing a helmet when you ride a bike. If you ride a skateboard or scooter, you should also wear pads.

1. What is another name for the backbone?
2. What is a vertebra?
3. What do your ribs **not** protect?
4. There are 54 bones in your:
5. Do the bones in your arms, wrists, hands, and fingers protect any organs?
6. What is the name of the bone between your pelvis and your knee?
7. What does your pelvis **not** do?

8. Name a part of your body that has a joint that moves like the hinge in a door.

9. What do your bones need that you can get by eating yogurt and other dairy products?

Part C- Review

Directions: Look at the poster below and then answer the questions.

Lost dog
Reward!

Our chocolate lab was lost near the corner of 3rd Ave and North Street on Wednesday. He ran after a squirrel when on a walk. He answers to the name **Sparky** and has a red and white collar.

$100 Reward

Please call 555-1234 if you find Sparky. We are miserable without him!

1. What number should you call if you find Sparky?

_____

2. How much reward money would you get if you found Sparky?

_____

3. Is this passage fiction or nonfiction?

_____

4. What color do you think a "chocolate lab" is?

    a. brown

    b. gray

    c. spotted

    d. black

5. What does Sparky's collar look like?

    a. polka dot

    b. brown and white

    c. red and white

    d. blue

6. In this poster, <u>miserable</u> means:

_____

7. Put an X next to each statement that is a small *detail* from the poster about a lost dog.
    1. _____ Sparky was lost when he tried to chase a squirrel.
    2. _____ The name of the lost dog is Sparky.
    3. _____ Sparky's favorite toy is a plastic hot dog.
    4. _____ Sparky is a chocolate lab.
    5. _____ Sparky has a red and white collar.

Part D Bonus

Funny poems called **limericks** have been around since the Middle Ages. But, in 1846 Edward Lear wrote a book of **limericks** called *Book of Nonsense*. He called his **limericks** "nonsense verse" because they were silly stories to make people laugh. **Limericks** became very popular thanks to Edward Lear. It is fun and easy to write your own **limericks**.

BONUS REVIEW

When you **classify details**, that helps you find out what a passage is **mostly about**.

A **biography** written by the person who the book is about is called an **autobiography**. Both **biography** and **autobiography** are **nonfiction**.

Lesson 49

Part A- Pronouns and Classification

Directions: Read the paragraph below, and then answer the questions.

The most difficult student that Mrs. Kraft ever had was Tommy McGuire. He had more energy than a generator in a dam. He couldn't sit still for more than a couple of seconds. Wherever you looked, it seems like you saw him. He raced everywhere he went. Tommy often crashed into other students when he shot down the hall. His teacher said he was a challenge, but he was a nice boy and everyone liked him, anyway.

How many times is Tommy's *name* mentioned in this paragraph? _____

How many times do pronouns refer to Tommy? _____

Part B- Pronouns and Classification (Continued)

Directions: After reading the details from the passage about Tommy, classify the items in the lists.

1. had great energy
   couldn't sit still
   raced everywhere
   shot down the hall
   These things show that Tommy was:

   a. a good boy

   b. Mrs. Kraft's favorite student

   c. active

   d. a poor student

Part C - Reading Subject Matter Books

Directions: Quickly read the chapter below, and then answer the questions.

Introduction

The 206 bones in our bodies have important purposes. Our organs and other tissues are attached to our bones. Bones protect organs such as the heart, the brain, and the lungs. Some of our bones make blood cells. Finally, bones store **minerals** (MIN er uls) that we need, such as **calcium** (CAL see um).

The Skull

The bones in your head are referred to as your **skull** (skul). Most of those bones protect your brain. The bones you can feel at the top of your head, in the back, and on the sides are the ones that protect your brain.

Other bones in the skull make up your face. Under your eyes, you can feel the holes in the bones where your eyes are. The only bone in your head that moves is your lower **jaw** (jaw). That bone makes it possible for you to chew food and to open and close your mouth.

The smallest bone in your whole body is in your head. That is the **stirrup** (STIR up) bone, which is right behind your eardrum. That tiny bone is only about 1/10 of an inch long.

The Spine

Another name for your spine is "backbone." There are really 25 different bones that make up our backbones. Each bone is called a **vertebra** (VER tuh bruh). When you touch the middle of your back, you can feel some of those bones.

Our spines help us to stand up straight. They also let us twist and bend. The most important job of the backbone is to protect the **spinal cord** (SPY nul kord). The spinal cord is made from many nerves. Nerves send messages between your brain and the rest of your body. The spinal cord goes right down the middle of the bones in the spine. The **vertebrae** (VER tuh bray; plural for vertebra) have small pads between them. The pads are like pillows between each vertebra. They keep the vertebrae from rubbing against each other.

The Ribs

Your ribs are like a cage. They protect special **organs** (OR guns) in your body. The most important organs that the ribs protect are your heart, your lungs, and your liver.

You can feel your ribs along the sides and front of your chest. When you take a deep breath, you can see the ribs in your chest. You have one set of ribs in the front and one in the back. Most people have 12 pairs of ribs. They are all attached to the vertebra in your spine. Some of them attach to the **sternum** (STIR num). The sternum is a hard bone in the middle of your chest.

Hands and Arms

There are three bones in each of your arms. There are *fifty-four* bones in the wrists and hands. That includes all the bones in your fingers. Those bones don't protect organs like the ribs do. They let you to do many activities, though. It is not even possible to name them all. When you type, play a sport, swing on a swing, or scratch your head, you're using your arms, wrists, and hands.

Your arm has two big bones between your elbow and your hand. They are called the **radius** (RAY dee us) and the **ulna** (UL nuh). There is just one big bone between your shoulder and your elbow. It is called the **humerus** (HYOU mer us). Eight small bones at the end of the radius and ulna make up your wrist. The middle part of each hand has five bones. There are two bones in each thumb. There are three bones in each finger. All those bones in your wrist, hands, and fingers are able to move.

Legs and Feet

Your leg bones are large. They have to be big because they support the weight of your whole body. The biggest bones in your body are between your **pelvis** (PELL vus) and your knees. That bone is called a femur (FEE mer). The tops of the femurs are attached to the pelvis. The pelvis bones are shaped like a circle. The pelvis holds up your spine. It also protects some parts of your digestive system and other organs.

You have two more bones in the bottom part of each leg. They are called the **tibia** (TIB ee uh) and the **fibula** (FIB you luh). Your ankles and feet are attached to those bones. There are seven bones in your ankle. Each foot has five bones. Your big toes have two bones each. The rest of your toes have three small bones each. The total number of bones in both feet, ankles, and toes, is 52.

We can't forget about your kneecap. The name of that bone is the **patella** (PAH tell uh). That bone is shaped like a triangle. It protects the knee joint.

You couldn't stand up, walk, run, or jump without all those bones in your legs, ankles, feet, and toes. The shape of your feet helps you stand up straight and keep your balance.

Moving Joints

The area where two bones meet is called a **joint** (JOYNT). Many of our joints move. That is what helps us move. Some joints work just like a door. You can close your arm and open it, like closing and opening a door. Most doors open and close in just one direction. Your arms and legs open and close in just one direction too.

The joints in your shoulders and hips are different. Those joints have a ball inside a **socket** (SOCK ut). That kind of joint lets you move your shoulders and hips in many directions.

The bones in your joints don't rub against each other. They are attached to each other with **ligaments** (LIG uh ments). Ligaments are very strong and flexible. They also help hold some organs in place. Your joints have a kind of liquid in them that helps the bones move smoothly. That is a lot like putting oil on a door to make it open and close better.

Taking Care of Your Bones

Your bones protect you and help you. You should take care of them. One way of taking care of your bones is to eat and drink foods that are good for you. Food helps you grow strong, healthy bones. Milk, low-fat cheese, yogurt, and ice cream have all the calcium your bones need. Most people don't mind eating ice cream to make their bones strong.

The other way to take care of your bones is to protect them. You should wear the right protection for different kinds of sports and activities. When you play football or hockey you need a helmet and pads for protection. Remember how your skull protects your brain? You should help out by always wearing a helmet when you ride a bike. If you ride a skateboard or scooter, you should also wear pads.

1. What is another name for the backbone?

_____

2. What is a vertebra?

_____

3. What do your ribs **not** protect?

    a.   heart

    b.   lungs

    c.   liver

    d.   stomach

4. There are 54 bones in your:

_____

5. Do the bones in your arms, wrists, hands, and fingers protect any organs?

_____

6. What is the name of the bone between your pelvis and your knee?

_____

7. What does your pelvis **not** do?

   a. protects some digestive and other organs

   b. gives your arms support

   c. connects to your spine

   d. connects to your femur

8. Name a part of your body that has a joint that moves like the hinge in a door.

_____

9. What do your bones need that you can get by eating yogurt and other dairy products?

_____

Part D Bonus

Limerick will be a bonus item on quizzes and tests that you take. A **limerick** is a funny poem with all lines having the same rhyme scheme. Lines 1, 2, and 5 rhyme with each other. Lines 3 and 4 rhyme with each other. Read one of Edward Lear's **limericks** below:

> There was an old man of Peru,
>
> Who watched his wife making a stew;
>
> But once by mistake,
>
> In a stove she did bake,
>
> That unfortunate man of Peru.

BONUS REVIEW

When you **classify details**, that helps you find out what a passage is **mostly about**.

Remember, a **biography** is a **nonfiction** story about someone's life.

When you read, you often have to **infer** something that isn't told to you directly in the passage.

Lesson 51

Part A - Reading Subject Matter Books

You have read two chapters from a book called *General Science Today*. One was on muscles and the other was on the skeletal system. You have gone through these steps:

1. You looked at the table of contents and answered questions that helped you to see what you already knew about the chapters.

2. You pronounced the words from the chapters that are in bold print, **like this**.

3. You read just the *first paragraph* under each heading in both chapters. Those paragraphs told you what the chapters were mostly about.

4. You studied the questions at the end of both chapters, before you actually read the whole chapter. That helps you notice important facts in a chapter.

5. You read a whole chapter, but you looked at the questions at the end of the chapter again before you read.

6. Finally, you read the chapter quickly and answered the questions at the end.

If you always follow steps like these when you read a textbook chapter, the chapter will be easier to read, the questions will be easier to answer, and you'll remember facts from the chapter better.

Beginning with Part B of this lesson, you will follow those steps, but some of them will be combined. You have to do some things on your own.

Part B - Reading Subject Matter Books (Continued)

Look at the table of contents for Chapter 3 on the nervous system. Your teacher will ask you what you might already know about the nervous system.

Name of Book: General Science Today

Table of Contents:

Unit 1...............Classification of Animals

Part C- Reading Subject Matter Books - Word Pronunciation

Directions: Below are some vocabulary words from a book chapter about the nervous system. Your teacher will read each word for you and then will ask you to pronounce it.

1. **automatic** (au toe MA tik)

2. **axons** (ax onz)

3. **brain stem**

4. **central**

5. **dendrites** (DEN drytz)

6. **nerves** (nurvz)

7. **nervous** (NER vuss) **system**

8. **neurons** (NER onz)

9. **peripheral** (per IF er el)

10. **spinal** (SPI nel) **cord**

Part D- Review

Directions: Read the passage, and then answer the questions.

How much do you know about ecology (e KOL ojy)? Ecology is the study of plants and animals and how they live. Ecologists study the different biomes in the world. A biome is an area that shares the same weather, animals, and plants. I think that one of the most interesting biomes is the rainforest.

There are two kinds of rainforests: temperate and tropical. You have probably heard of tropical rainforests before. They are found in Central and South America, Australia, Asia, and Africa. Even though rainforests are all over the world, they only make up 6-7% of the land on earth. Tropical rainforests are warm and wet all year long. They are wet because they get 80 to 400 inches of rain a year.

Temperate rainforests also get a lot of rain. They are <u>damp</u> throughout the whole year. They get 60 to 200 inches of rain a year. Temperate rainforests have more fog than tropical rainforests. That is because they are cooler. Most temperate rainforests are found on the Pacific coast of North America.

Both temperate and tropical rainforests have many interesting plants and animals. One kind of flower is called an orchid. There are more than 20,000 kinds of orchids in the rainforest. Half of all the kinds of plants and animals on earth live in tropical rainforests. That is a lot of different plants and animals!

1. According to the passage, how much rain falls in a tropical rainforest?

2. Which kind of rainforest gets a lot of fog?

_____

3. Is this passage fiction or nonfiction?

_____

4. Where are most temperate rainforests located?

_____

5. Why do you think it is important to protect the rainforests?

    a. because people like to vacation there

    b. because half the species of plants and animals live there

    c. because they give ecologists something to study

    d. because we need rain

6. In this passage, <u>damp</u> means:

_____

7. Put an X next to each statement that is a small *detail* from the passage about rainforests.

    1. _____ It's hard to vacation in the rainforest since there aren't any hotels.

    2. _____ There are two kinds of rainforests.

    3. _____ Tropical rainforests are found all over the world.

    4. _____ Many different species of plants and animals live in the rainforest.

    5. _____ Ecologists study biomes.

Part E - Bonus Review

Fiction comes from the imagination of the writer. Sometimes, it is hard to tell if a story is true or made up.

An **autobiography** is the story of someone's life, written by that person.

A **detail** is a small part of something. In a passage, there are a lot of small details.

Lesson 52

Part A- Pronouns and Classification

Directions: Read the paragraph below, and then answer the questions.

Some dogs make great watch dogs. My dog Melissa is not one of those dogs. She loves all people no matter who they are. We tried to get her to bark at strangers, but she only barks when the doorbell rings. When we answer the door, Melissa wags her tail at the stranger. If a stranger comes into the house, she lays on her back for a belly rub. On walks, Melissa likes to greet all the dogs she sees. She also gives the people she sees a tail wag and a big lick. She will never make it as a watch dog!

How many times is the dog's name, Melissa, mentioned in this paragraph? _____

How many times do pronouns refer to Melissa? _____

Part B- Pronouns and Classification (Continued)

Directions: After reading the details from the passage about Melissa the dog, classify the items in the lists.

1. won't bark at strangers
   greets people with a tail wag and a big lick
   loves all people no matter who they are
   wags her tails at strangers
   These things show that Melissa is:

   a. a very friendly dog

   b. a large dog

   c. a mean dog

   d. a good watch dog

Part C - Reading Subject Matter Books

Directions: Read the questions below from the end of the science chapter on nerves, and then close your workbook.

1. The human nervous system is more powerful than:
2. What do we call the brain and spinal cord?
3. What does your spine protect?
4. Nerves attach to how many senses?
5. What sends messages from your ears to your brain?
6. The part of your nervous system that works without you thinking about it is called what?
7. What connects your brain to your spinal cord?
8. How do you know when something touches your skin?
9. What does not help you take care of your brain and nervous system?

Part D- Review

Directions: Look at the invitation below and then answer the questions.

You're invited!

To a Presidents' Day Costume Party!

On Saturday, February 17th at 7:00 p.m.
At Andy Olivier's house
5 Main Street
Newtown
(Directions on Reverse)

Please dress up as your favorite president. Select your costume carefully because there will be a prize for the person with the best costume!

Everyone please bring a snack to share!

---

1. According to the invitation, where is the Presidents' Day party?

_____

2. What time is the party?

_____

3. Who do you think will be a judge for the costume contest?

    a. one of the kids at the party

    b. Andy's two cats

    c. Andy's baby brother

    d. Andy's parents

4. Why do you think Andy put the directions to his house on the other side of the invitation?

    a. everyone may not know how to get to his house

    b. because kids can't drive

    c. because he has no friends

    d. he wants everyone to be on time

5. What should you bring to the party?

_____

6. In this passage, <u>select</u> means:

_____

Part E - Bonus Review

Remember that all the words below are **pronouns**:

I	me	my
you	him	your
it	us	its
she	their	her
he	they	his
we	them	our

Limericks are funny poems. All limericks have five lines and the same rhythm.

The rhythm in lines 1, 2, and 5 usually sounds like this: da DUM da da DUM da da DUM da. Lines 3 and 4 sound like this: da da DUM da da DUM.

Be careful to *spell* limerick correctly: **l-i-m-e-r-i-c-k.**

Lesson 53

Part A- Vocabulary

Directions: After you read each model, choose the word from the list that could *best* replace the underlined word in the model sentence.

1. **Model:** When Adam's best friend was hurt in a car crash, Adam made a <u>vow</u> to do everything he could to stop drunk driving. Now Adam volunteers for a group that fights drunk driving.

    a. appointment

    b. wish

    c. promise

    d. call

2. **Model:** Last winter we got stuck travelling in a storm. We had to stay in the airport overnight. When we finally got home, we were <u>weary</u>, but happy to be safe.

    a. late

    b. glad

    c. sick

    d. tired

Part B- Reading Subject Matter Books

Directions: Below is all of Chapter 3 from Unit 2 of the book, *General Science Today*. You are not going to read the whole chapter in today's lesson.

Instead, you are just going to read *the first paragraph* after each heading. After you read the first paragraph after a heading, answer the questions for that paragraph.

The first paragraph and the questions for that paragraph are in boxes.

Introduction

Your muscles and bones help protect another important system in your body. That system is called the **nervous** (NER vuss) system. The nervous system controls your heartbeat and breathing. In fact, it controls all your body systems.

1. What protects the nervous system?

_____

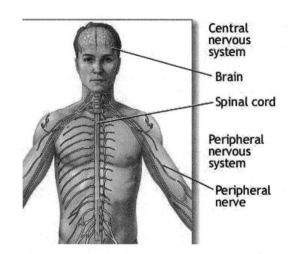

You can think of the nervous system as a computer that controls what goes on in your body. The nervous system is even more powerful than the biggest computer! There are three parts of the nervous system.

Central Nervous System

The **central nervous system** is made up of the brain and the **spinal** (SPI nel) cord. Messages move from the brain to the spinal cord. Then messages move to **nerves** (nurvz), and back to the brain.

2. Which **two** things make up the central nervous system?

    a. heart

    b. brain

    c. spinal cord

The brain controls all voluntary muscle movements. Balance, feelings, and habits are also controlled by the brain. The brain is protected by the skull.

The spinal cord is made of many nerves. These nerves run from the bottom of the brain all the way down your back. The spinal cord is protected by your backbone, or spine.

Peripheral Nervous System

Nerves run from the brain to the spinal cord. Nerves also branch out to every part of your body. You can think of these nerves as phone wires. They send messages to all the different parts of your body. These nerves are called the **peripheral** (per IF er el) nervous system.

3. What is the peripheral nervous system made out of?

_____

There are special nerve cells for each of your five senses. You have nerve cells that pick up sounds. These nerves send a message from your ears to your brain. They tell your brain that you are hearing something. You also have nerves that work with your other senses. There are special nerves for seeing, feeling, touching, and tasting.

Automatic Nervous System

The **automatic** (au tu MA tik) nervous system makes things happen in your body even while you are sleeping. The automatic nervous system is made up of the spinal cord and the **brain stem**.

4. What body system controls things that happen in your body without you thinking about them?

_____

5. What **two** body parts make up the automatic nervous system?

    a.   spinal cord

    b.   bladder

    c.   brain stem

Your brain stem is at the very bottom of your brain. It is just above your neck. The brain stem connects your brain to your spinal cord. The brain stem controls all involuntary muscle movements.

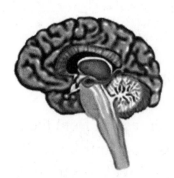

Your heart beating is an involuntary muscle movement. Breathing and digestion are involuntary too. You don't have to think about breathing, it just happens. Your automatic nervous system is taking care of it for you.

Nerves

The brain, spinal cord, and nerves make up the nervous system. Nerves are like wires inside your body. You know when something touches you. The nerves in your skin tell you. They send signals to your brain. The nerves tell your brain if something is hot, cold, hard, or soft.

6. How do you know when something touches your skin?

_____

7. Nerves are like:

    a.   street signs

    b.   telephone poles

    c.   wires

Nerves are made of individual cells called **neurons** (NER onz). The brain and spinal cord are made of billions of neurons. Neurons have fibers that reach out to other nerves. Fibers called **axons** (ax onz) *send out* signals to other neurons.

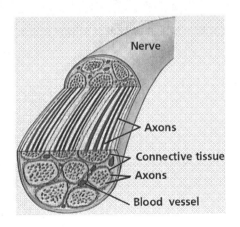

Fibers called **dendrites** (DEN drytz) *get* signals from other neurons.

You are born with all the neurons you will ever need. Many of the neurons are not used when you are young. Neuron fibers connect to each other when you learn things.

Taking Care of Your Nervous System

You need to take care of your nervous system. You wouldn't be able to do anything without your brain! You can take care of your nervous system by eating healthy foods. You also need to get enough sleep and exercise. Your brain works very hard during the day. It needs to rest at night when you sleep. Your brain needs good foods to keep it going all day long.

8.   What are two things you can do to keep your nervous system healthy?

_____

You also need to protect your brain by wearing a helmet when you ride a bike or play sports. You should always wear your seat belt in the car. Your seat belt will protect your brain and spinal cord if you get in an accident. Learning new things is like exercise for your brain. Your brain and nervous system like to work hard. Working hard keeps them healthy and strong. Learn something new every day for a healthy brain!

Part C - Bonus Review

An **inference** question is one you have to answer by reading a passage and also using information you already know.

When you **classify details**, you figure out what is similar about the **details** you are **classifying**.

Lesson 54

Part A- Vocabulary (Matching)

Directions: Find the definitions from the box that match the words below.

```
a.   nervous

b.   pick

c.   promise

d.   try

e.   tired
```

Write the letter of the definition that matches each word.

1. select _____

2. tense _____

3. weary _____

4. attempt _____

5. vow _____

Part B- Pronouns and Classification

Directions: Read the paragraph below, and then answer the questions.

Every class has a class clown. My dad was the class clown when he was in school. Now, he is the clown of the whole family. His name is Dan, so we call him "Dan the joke man." He knows a million jokes. He always thinks of the right one to make you feel better if you're feeling down. All my friends even think he is funny. They love his jokes. They really love the impressions he does of famous people. Sometimes he even does crazy stuff just to make us laugh. The whole family really appreciates him, especially when one of us has a bad day.

How many times is the author's dad mentioned in this paragraph by "my dad" or by his name? _____

How many times do pronouns refer to the author's dad? _____

Part C- Pronouns and Classification (Continued)

Directions: After reading the details from the passage about the author's dad, classify the items in the lists.

1. is called "Dan the joke man"
    was the class clown
    knows a million jokes
    does impressions of famous people
    These things show that the author's dad is:

    a. friendly

    b. smart

    c. loving

    d. funny

Part D- Review

Directions: Look at the poster below and then answer the questions.

Science Club!

Sign Up Sheet

Do you enjoy science projects? Mr. Perez is starting a Science Club! Sign up below and come to the first meeting on **Thursday, September 20th at 3:30 p.m.** in the science lab to see what Science Club is all about!

1. _____
2. _____
3. _____
4. _____
5. _____
6. _____
7. _____
8. _____
9. _____
10. _____
11. _____
12. _____

1. According to the poster, who is starting a science club?

_____

2. When is the first science club meeting?

_____

3. Where is the first science club meeting?

_____

4. What do you think kids in science club will do when they meet?

    a.   art projects

    b.   science projects

    c.   talk about history

    d.   plan a soccer club

5. Why do you think Mr. Perez wants kids to sign up for science club before the first meeting?

    a.   to make sure he likes everyone who signs up

    b.   because the science lab only holds 6 people

    c.   so he can make sure that he has enough supplies for everyone

    d.   to make sure that only boys sign up

6. According to the poster, how many people can sign up for science club?

_____

7. Which belongs in box 2 below?

read the poster		come to the first meeting
1	2	3

    a.   sign up

    b.   do a science project

    c.   talk to Mr. Perez

Part E -Bonus

See if you can hear the rhythm in this **limerick** by Rudyard Kipling:

There   was   a   small boy   of   Quebec

da   DUM da   da   DUM da   da   DUM

Who was   buried   in   snow   to   his neck

da   da   DUM da   da   DUM   da   da DUM

When   they   said,   "Are   you   friz?"

da   da   DUM   da   da   DUM

He replied,   "Yes,   I   is —

da da DUM   da   da DUM

But   we   don't   call   this   cold   in Quebec"

da   da   DUM da   da   DUM   da   da DUM

Lesson 56

Part A- Main Idea

In this lesson you are going to combine what you have learned about counting pronouns and classifying details. By combining these skills, you will learn to determine the main idea of a passage. A main idea is like a summary.

Part B- Main Idea (Continued)

Directions: Read the paragraph below. Count the number of times that Darby's name is used in the passage, and then count the number of times that pronouns refer to Darby. Add those together.

My little kitten, Darby, is a handful. Once, Darby climbed up the drapes in our house. She tore them to pieces with her sharp claws. Another time, she got on the kitchen counter and knocked a box of sugar onto the floor. We bought her a litter box, but she doesn't always use it. I guess she doesn't know it is hers. You can imagine what a mess she might make. Sometimes my mom yells, "I think I'm going to sell Darby!" But Mom doesn't mean it. Darby is just too cute.

1. How many times is Darby's name mentioned in the passage? _____

2. How many times are pronouns used to refer to Darby? _____

3. The passage talks about Darby using both her name and pronouns how many times? _____

Part C- Main Idea (Continued)

Directions: After reading the details from the passage in Part B about Darby, classify these details from the passage.

1. tore the drapes to pieces
   knocked a box of sugar onto the floor
   doesn't always use her litter box
   Mom yells
   These things show that Darby:

    a.   is not too smart

    b.   is in trouble a lot

    c.   is cute

    d.   is not very active

Part D- Main Idea (Continued)

Now that you know how often Darby is talked about in the Part B passage, and you have classified the details, you are ready to make a main idea statement. By filling in the boxes below with the information you figured out in Parts B and C, you will have a good main idea statement:

First: Identify who or what is talked about the most in the Part B passage.	Then: Classify what is being said about the person or thing.

That is your main idea statement! "Darby is in trouble a lot."

A good main idea statement:

1. Tells who or what is talked about most
2. Classifies the details in the passage

NOTE: A detail from a passage is never a main idea statement.

Part E - Bonus Review

Remember, a **detail** is a small part of something.

Also remember that **inference** is when you guess about something from another thing that you already know.

Lesson 57

Part A - Vocabulary (Matching)

Directions: Find the definitions from the box that match the words below.

a.	very bad
b.	smart
c.	let go
d.	hurt
e.	long hole

Write the letter of the definition that matches each word.

1. intelligent _____

2. ditch _____

3. horrible _____

4. release _____

5. ache _____

Part B - Reading Subject Matter Books

For the chapter on nerves from *General Science Today*, you have gone through the following steps so far:

1. You looked at the table of contents and answered questions that helped you to see what you already knew about the chapter.

2. You pronounced the words from the chapter that are in bold print, **like this**.

3. You read just the *first paragraph* under each heading in the chapter. Those paragraphs told you what the chapters were mostly about.

In this lesson, you are going to study the questions at the end of the chapter, before you actually read the whole chapter. That will help you notice important facts in the chapter.

Part C- Reading Subject Matter Books (Continued)

Directions: Read the questions below from the end of the science chapter on nerves, and then close your workbook.

1. The brain and what else make up the central nervous system?
2. What does your spine protect?
3. What sends messages to your brain from every part of your body?
4. How many senses do you have?
5. Here are two senses we have: hearing and touch. What are the other senses?
6. What is at the very bottom of the brain?
7. What automatically takes care of things like breathing and digestion for you?
8. What is each individual cell in a nerve called?
9. What should you do to protect your brain when you're riding a bike, a skate board, or a scooter?
10. One thing you can do to keep your nervous system healthy is exercise. What two other things does your brain need to keep healthy?

Part D- Review

Directions: Read the passage, and then answer the questions.

Can you believe there was a time when there were no women doctors? The first woman doctor was Elizabeth Blackwell in 1849.

Elizabeth Blackwell was born in 1821 in England. She moved with her family to America when she was 11. After her father died, Elizabeth, her mother, and her sisters opened a private school. While Elizabeth was teaching, she decided that she wanted to go to medical school and become a doctor.

Elizabeth knew that it would be hard to get a medical school to teach a woman. She applied to many schools. She hoped that she would get into one. Only one school agreed to teach her. At Geneva Medical College in New York, the students voted on whether Elizabeth should be able to go to school there. The students thought the vote was a joke. They voted to let her go to school there. Elizabeth was not joking. She graduated first in her class two years later.

After school, Elizabeth trained in Paris. While she was in Paris, an infection <u>injured</u> her eye. She became blind in that eye so she couldn't become a surgeon. When she came back to America she became a doctor. She helped mostly women and children. Later, she helped start a medical college for women. Elizabeth Blackwell made other women want to become doctors too.

1. According to the passage, what medical school did Elizabeth Blackwell go to?

_____

2. What year was Elizabeth Blackwell born?

_____

3. Is this passage fiction or nonfiction?

_____

4. Why do you think Elizabeth's eye injury kept her from becoming a surgeon?

    a. she was too sick

    b. she was too old

    c. surgeons need perfect eyesight

    d. she didn't want to do more training

5. How do you think Elizabeth felt when no medical school would teach her?

    a. tired

    b. happy

    c. frustrated

    d. scared

6. Look at the third paragraph of the passage. Count how many times pronouns are used to refer to Elizabeth Blackwell.

_____

7. In this passage, <u>injured</u> means:

_____

8. Which belongs in box 2 below?

becomes a teacher		becomes a doctor
1	2	3

   a.   becomes blind in one eye

   b.   tries to get into medical school

   c.   helps to start a medical school for women

9. Put an X next to each statement that is a small *detail* from the passage about Elizabeth Blackwell.

   1. _____ Elizabeth trained in Paris.

   2. _____ Elizabeth Blackwell was born in England.

   3. _____ Elizabeth wanted to become a surgeon.

   4. _____ Elizabeth had four brothers and four sisters.

   5. _____ Elizabeth graduated from Geneva Medical College.

Part E - Bonus Review

Remember that every well-written paragraph or passage is **mostly about** one thing.

Fiction is a type of writing created from the imagination of the writer. Fiction isn't from history or fact. When writing is true or factual it is called **nonfiction**.

Lesson 58

Part A - Vocabulary (Matching)

Directions: Find the definitions from the box that match the words below.

a.	round
b.	very old
c.	bothers
d.	skin
e.	mix

Write the letter of the definition that matches each word.

1. flesh _____

2. irritates _____

3. ancient _____

4. blend _____

5. circular _____

Part B- Main Idea (Continued)

Directions: Read the paragraph below. Count the number of times that Marty's name is used in the passage, and then count the number of times that pronouns refer to Marty. Add those together.

Marty walked out his front door and looked down the road. He saw dark clouds forming in the sky. They were headed in the direction of his house. Marty was not worried. In fact, he liked to watch lightning flash. He also enjoyed the loud blast of thunder. Marty stayed on his porch. He wanted to see the free show the storm was giving.

1. How many times is Marty's name mentioned in the passage? _____

2. How many times are pronouns used to refer to Marty? _____

3. The passage talks about Marty using both his name and pronouns how many times? _____

Part C - Main Idea (Continued)

Directions: After reading the details from the passage in Part B about Marty, classify these details from the passage.

1. saw dark clouds forming
   liked to watch lightning
   enjoyed the thunder
   stayed outside to see the free show
   These things show that Marty enjoyed:

   a. the porch

   b. daydreaming

   c. watching a storm

   d. loud noises

Part D- Main Idea (Continued)

Now that you know how often Marty is talked about in the Part B passage, and you have classified the details, you are ready to make a main idea statement. By filling in the boxes below with the information you figured out in Parts B and C, you will have a good main idea statement:

First: Identify who or what is talked about the most in the Part B passage.	Then: Classify what is being said about the person or thing.

That is your main idea statement! "Marty watched a storm."

A good main idea statement:

1. Tells who or what is talked about most
2. Classifies the details in the passage

NOTE: A detail from a passage is never a main idea statement.

Part E - Bonus Review

Pronouns refer to people or things. All the words below are **pronouns**:

I	me	my
you		your
it		its
she	her	her
he	him	his
we	us	our
they	them	their

Remember, a **biography** is a **nonfiction** story about someone's life. A **biography** written by the person who the book is about is called an **autobiography**.

Lesson 59

Part A - Main Idea (Continued)

Directions: Read the paragraph below. Count the number of times that John and Joe's names are used in the passage, and then count the number of times that pronouns refer to John and Joe. Add those together.

John and Joe were good friends. After spending part of the summer together, they became even closer. They had great times hiking, canoeing, swimming, and riding horses. Sometimes in the evening, they sat around the campfire. If the night was warm, John and Joe would sleep outside. Every week they would write postcards home to their parents. Once, their parents came to visit them for the weekend. John and Joe hoped they could do this every summer.

1. How many times are John and Joe's names mentioned in the passage? _____

2. How many times are pronouns used to refer to John and Joe? _____

3. The passage talks about John and Joe using both their names and pronouns how many times? _____

Part B - Main Idea (Continued)

Directions: After reading the details from the passage in Part A about John and Joe, classify these details from the passage.

1. spent the summer together

   hiked, canoed, swam, and rode horses

   sat around the campfire

   slept outside

   These things show that John and Joe enjoyed:

   a. going to summer camp together

   b. going on family vacations

   c. having an adventure in the winter

   d. visiting their grandparents

Part C- Main Idea (Continued)

Now that you know how often John and Joe are talked about in the Part A passage, and you have classified the details, you are ready to make a main idea statement. By filling in the boxes below with the information you figured out in Parts A and B, you will have a good main idea statement:

First: Identify who or what is talked about the most in the Part A passage.	Then: Classify what is being said about the person or thing.

That is your main idea statement! "John and Joe went to camp together."

A good main idea statement:

1. Tells who or what is talked about most
2. Classifies the details in the passage

NOTE: A detail from a passage is never a main idea statement.

Part D - Bonus Review

When you **classify details**, that helps you find out what a passage is **mostly about**.

Limericks are funny poems. All **limericks** have five lines and the same rhyming pattern.